GREAT LIVES OBSERVED

Gerald Emanuel Stearn, *General Editor*

EACH VOLUME IN THE SERIES VIEWS THE CHARACTER AND ACHIEVEMENT OF A GREAT WORLD FIGURE IN THREE PERSPECTIVES—THROUGH HIS OWN WORDS, THROUGH THE OPINIONS OF HIS CONTEMPORARIES, AND THROUGH RETROSPECTIVE JUDGMENTS—THUS COMBINING THE INTIMACY OF AUTOBIOGRAPHY, THE IMMEDIACY OF EYEWITNESS OBSERVATION, AND THE OBJECTIVITY OF MODERN SCHOLARSHIP.

JOHN B. RAE, *the editor of this volume in the Great Lives Observed series, is Professor of History and Chairman of the Department of Humanities and Social Sciences at Harvey Mudd College. He is author of* The United States in World History, An Early American Industrial Community *and several other books, including two volumes on the American automobile industry. He has also written many articles and reviews.*

GREAT LIVES OBSERVED

Henry
FORD

Edited by JOHN B. RAE

With all the millions, with all the powers, with all the successes;
with all the knotty problems solved and forgotten, one somehow
gets the impression of a man groping, struggling, trying to adjust
to a universe that is tragically inadjustable.

—GAMALIEL BRADFORD

A SPECTRUM BOOK

PRENTICE-HALL, INC., ENGLEWOOD CLIFFS, N.J.

The quotation on the title page is from
Gamaliel Bradford, "Henry Ford," *The Quick
and the Dead* (Boston, 1931).

Copyright © 1969 by PRENTICE-HALL, INC.;
Englewood Cliffs, New Jersey.

A SPECTRUM BOOK

Current printing (last number): 10 9 8 7 6 5 4 3 2 1

P 13-386599-1

C 13-386607-6

Library of Congress Catalog Card Number: 69-15348

Printed in the United States of America

Prentice-Hall International, Inc. (*London*)

Acknowledgments

I have had much generous assistance and cooperation in the task of compiling this book. I wish to express my particular gratitude to Dr. Henry E. Edmunds and the staff of the Ford Archives; Mr. Richard Ruddell, Manager, Educational Affairs Department, Ford Motor Company; and Mrs. James J. Bradley, Head, Automotive History Collection, the Detroit Public Library. All have gone out of their way to assist me in locating materials.

JOHN B. RAE

Contents

PART ONE
FORD SPEAKS TO THE WORLD

1
The Early Steps   12

The First Fords, *13*   The Car for the Great Multitude, *17*

2
On Business   20

"The Price Was Too High," *20*   "A Reasonable Profit—But Not Too Much," *27*   Business Versus Finance, *28*   Markets, Prices, and Mass Production, *31*

3
Labor and Wages   35

Ford Labor Policies; The Futility of Strikes, *35*   Employers and Employees: The Single Standard, *40*

4
Economic Ideas   44

Power, Money, and Poverty, *44*   The Economic Significance of the Automobile, *50*

5
War and History   53

"History Is More Or Less Bunk," *53*   Ford Testimony, July 15, 1919, *54*   "A United States of the World," *54* viii

Introduction

Henry Ford's lifetime spanned the growth of American industry from childhood to maturity. When he was born in 1863, the United States was just on the threshold of large-scale industrial development. The output of its factories was quantitatively and, for the most part, qualitatively behind Great Britain and France. When he died in 1947, the electronic computer had come into existence and industry was moving toward automation. In industrial capacity the United States held a commanding lead, and its production techniques were the model for others to emulate.

The seeds of this metamorphosis were clearly germinating in 1863. By that time American manufacturing methods had already acquired a distinctive character because of the American propensity to use machines rather than human labor whenever possible. As early as 1850 the machine production of standardized parts was known as "the American system of manufacturing." There had been a number of experiments with such processes in Europe, antedating the American experience, but they were not generally accepted. The reasons are complex; the essential difference is that even in technologically advanced Western Europe it was still frequently more economical to use labor-intensive rather than capital-intensive techniques, whereas the opposite was generally true for North America with its sparser population.

As a young man Ford witnessed the phenomenal industrial growth of the post-Civil War period: the rise of giant organizations like Carnegie's empire in steel and Rockefeller's in oil, and the extension of the railroad network across the continent. It was an era of rapid technological change with apparently limitless opportunity for men with business acumen or mechanical talent. It was also an era of paradox in that the economic growth appeared to be of limited benefit to common men. Farm life continued to be isolated, monotonous, and usually unprofitable. The industrial worker was saddled with long hours and low wages. It also remained generally true that for the ordinary individual, despite the great advance represented by the railroad and the steamship, travel over any distance was difficult, uncomfortable, and expensive.

Ford's career impinged on all these problems. His policy of high wages and an eight-hour day, when most industries still worked ten or twelve, was a novel step in industrial relations, and the mass production of motor

1

vehicles so as to put an automobile within the reach of practically everyone gave a previously unattainable freedom of movement to farm and city dweller alike. The great bulk of the literature on Henry Ford is concerned with the nature and extent of his contributions in these fields. There are markedly differing interpretations of what Ford himself actually accomplished. The rise and decline of a Ford legend can be readily traced. When he achieved his first great successes he was hailed as the prophet of a new era and as an infallible authority on practically everything. But then he lost his industrial ascendancy and displayed a quite obvious fallibility in other matters. He never lost his prestige entirely, but during the New Deal his long and bitter resistance to organized labor gave ample scope for his critics. After his death came reappraisal and at least partial rehabilitation. The opening of the Ford Archives and the monumental study made by Allan Nevins and his associates have permitted an accurate evaluation of Ford's work. His personality, however, continues to elude us: was he a simple man erroneously assumed to be complex, or an enormously complex individual with a misleading aura of simplicity?

Henry Ford was born on July 30, 1863, the son of William Ford, a prosperous farmer of Dearborn, Michigan. Young Henry remained on the farm until he was 16, by which time he was aware that he disliked farm work and was fascinated by machinery. He walked to nearby Detroit, served an apprenticeship with the James Flower and Brothers Machine Shop, and then worked for the Detroit Drydock Company and Westinghouse. In 1886 he went back to Dearborn and settled on land offered by his father, who wanted him to become a farmer, but he stayed only two years, long enough to get married to Clara Bryant in 1887. During this time he built a steam tractor that proved unsuccessful and may have convinced him that steam power was unsuitable when he later turned his attention to motor vehicles.

Ford returned to Detroit in 1888 and went to work for the Detroit Illuminating (now Detroit Edison) Company, rising in a few years to be chief engineer. He also began to experiment with the idea of a horseless carriage. It is not clear just when he developed the idea or started to build a car; the work was certainly in progress in the early 1890's, but it is equally certain that Ford's first car was preceded not only by a number of European pioneers but by four Americans (the Duryeas, Elwood Haynes, Hiram Percy Maxim, and Charles B. King).

What was distinctive about Ford's "quadricycle" of 1896 was that it was the lightest (500 lbs.) of the pioneer American gasoline cars and therefore may indicate that Ford was already thinking of "a car for the great multitude." We do know that he had earlier contemplated manufacturing low-priced watches in quantity. If the dream was there, it was not yet ready to become a reality. Ford's first venture into the automobile business in 1899 was a failure, except that he attracted some attention to himself by building and driving racing cars. In the meantime others like Alexander Winton and Ransom E. Olds were establishing themselves as commercial producers of gasoline automobiles, and the Olds curved-dash buggy, the "Merry Oldsmobile," was actually the first quantity-produced, popular-priced American car.

Accordingly, when Ford was able to make a fresh start in 1903 by founding the Ford Motor Company, his venture must have seemed no different from the hundreds of others that were struggling to get into the growing motor vehicle industry. There have been over 1,500 separate firms in the American automobile industry, producing over three thousand makes of car, and there was little to distinguish the Ford firm from the others. It began with $28,000 in cash, mostly supplied by Alexander Y. Malcomson, a Detroit coal dealer, and its first models were very much like their competitors. Yet in five years Ford was one of the leading American manufacturers. Some of the credit is due to the extremely able assistants whom Henry Ford was able to attract: James S. Couzens, who was the company's business genius; C. H. Wills, a brilliant engineer; the Dodge brothers, who built the first Ford engines; and others. It seems only fair, however, to point out that Henry Ford controlled the company and was responsible for gathering this talented group.

In addition to ordinary competition, Ford had to meet the threat to his company offered by the Selden patent. This was a comprehensive patent on a "road engine" first applied for in 1879 by George B. Selden, an inventor and patent attorney of Rochester, New York, but not actually issued until 1895. The long delay was due to Selden's ability to utilize loopholes in the patent laws in order to postpone issue of his patent until it had some prospect of commercial value. Eventually he sold control of the patent to a syndicate known as the Electric Vehicle Company, which in turn reached an agreement with most of the principal automobile firms to administer a licensing system through an Association of Licensed Automobile Manufacturers. Ford was unable to secure a license and decided, along with some others, to fight. After eight years of litigation, the Selden patent was adjudged valid but not infringed, on the ground that it applied only to vehicles with engines based on the constant-pressure, two-cycle type which Selden had originally proposed. Far from damaging Ford, the Selden suit provided him with invaluable publicity, with Ford in the role of the small independent bravely challenging an attempt at monopoly. Actually, by the time the case ended David had become bigger than Goliath, but the favorable image had been established and it persisted.

The Selden case did not in the least impede the phenomenal advance of Henry Ford and the Ford Motor Company. They were helped by the fact that after the turn of the century the automobile rapidly caught the

imagination of the American public, unhampered by the gloomy predic-
tion made by Woodrow Wilson in 1906, when he was president of Prince-
ton University, that the motorcar would bring socialism to America by
inciting the poor to envy of the rich. There was a rising demand for automobiles, and a near-limitless potential market if cars could be built at a
price within the reach of the common man. Yet the attrition rate in the
automobile industry was high, and others besides Henry Ford were trying
to exploit the possibilities of the cheap car.

There is an extensive literature on the introduction of the Model T and
mass production by the Ford Motor Company, attempting to explain the
reasons for Ford's rise to ascendancy. What emerges is that, although
various individuals made indispensable contributions to Ford's success,
the fundamental decisions were made by Henry Ford himself. He had the
concept of "a car for the great multitude" when the Ford Motor Company
was established and he told one of his partners, "The way to make automobiles is to make one automobile like another automobile, to make them
all alike, to make them come from the factory just alike—just like one pin
is like another pin when it comes from the pin factory."

The first essential step was to design a car suitable for mass use rather
than one that could be manufactured cheaply. The Model T filled this
requirement—durable, easy to operate, economical to maintain—and in
1909 Ford consciously made the decision to build this car and no other.
Then came the search for a method of low-cost production, resulting in
the moving assembly line, which became completely operative early in
1914. This too involved a critical decision: whether to commit the company to a manufacturing technique that demanded a heavy investment
in tooling and would pay only if a volume of sales was attained beyond
anything so far experienced in the automobile industry. It makes no
difference whether the ideas originated with Henry Ford or someone
else: as president and majority stockholder of the Ford Motor Company
the final responsibility had to be his.

The assembly line was the culmination of the process of mechanization
and standardization which had been developing in American industry
since the time of Oliver Evans and Eli Whitney. The novel features of the
Ford system were that in order to have quantity production of a complex
mechanical device like a motor vehicle it was necessary to surpass anything
in previous practice in terms of synchronization, precision, and specialization.

The results were more successful than Ford and his associates could have
expected. The Ford Motor Company effectively reached the mass market;
within a few years it was producing half the automobiles in the world and
in the early 1920's reached a peak of sixty per cent of the motor vehicle
output of the United States. When the production feat was completed with

the introduction of a wage level of five dollars for an eight-hour day, Henry Ford became world-famous. He was widely regarded, with reasonable justification, as the prophet and oracle of a new industrial era. The mass-production techniques introduced by the Ford Motor Company were widely adopted by other industries in the United States and elsewhere; in Germany during the 1920's the process of reorganizing and rationalizing production was termed *fordismus*.

Now that Ford was a public figure, his opinions on every conceivable subject were eagerly sought, and he had little hesitation about expressing them. But in his public life he was rather less successful than in his industrial career. During World War I he allowed himself to be led into the "peace ship" episode, when he organized an expedition to sail to Europe in the *Oskar II* and persuade the belligerents to stop fighting. His anti-militarism also resulted in the *Chicago Tribune* calling him an anarchist, and the ensuing libel suit proved to be a humiliating experience for Henry Ford. Nevertheless he was proposed for political office and was quite seriously attracted by the prospect. He ran for United States Senator from Michigan on the Democratic ticket in 1918 and was narrowly defeated. His opponent, Truman Newberry, subsequently resigned his seat in the face of allegations of election frauds. Subsequently there was a Ford-for-President boom which found him temporarily responsive.

Ford's worst blunder in this phase of his career was undoubtedly the anti-Semitic campaign he permitted to be conducted by the *Dearborn Independent*, which he owned. He even resurrected the long-discredited forgery, the *Protocols of the Wise Men of Zion*, and published it as a valid historical document. When the result of the campaign was loss of business and threat of court action, Ford placed the blame on his faithful publicist, W. J. Cameron, and claimed that he had not known what was being said in his paper.

None of these displays of ineptitude affected Ford's stature in the eyes of the general public: he was still the industrial mircle worker. In the years immediately after World War I the Ford Motor Company seemed to be on a course of phenomenal growth. Ford weathered the depression of 1921 when other automobile firms were in serious trouble, and in the process staved off a threat of losing control of his company to bankers from whom he had borrowed. Even defeat in a lawsuit brought by his stockholders to compel the payment of special dividends was turned to Ford's advantage; he bought the stockholders out and the Ford family became sole owners of the company. There seemed to be no limit to what Ford could achieve. His company was a vast integrated enterprise with a conscious goal (never achieved) of becoming completely self-contained. He bought the ramshackle Detroit, Toledo, and Ironton Railroad and made it pay, although his critics asserted that this was achieved by using the heavy volume of Ford freight to secure special favors for the D.T. and I. from intersecting trunk lines.

But the seeds of decline were already present; indeed, the very quality of single-minded dedication to one basic idea that had accounted for Ford's rise now became a source of weakness. He gave the automobile to the common man, but once the common man became used to the idea of owning a car, he then aspired to have a better one, and this Ford did not provide. The Model T was the symbol of his success, and he would not give it up, despite the urging of his son Edsel and of William S. Knudsen. Knudsen, in fact, left the Ford Motor Company in 1921 because he could not convince Henry Ford that a model change was necessary.

Others, in the meantime, were not only imitating Ford's methods but improving on them. It became possible to buy a new car with more graceful styling and better equipment than the ungainly "Tin Lizzie" for one or two hundred dollars more and to get better quality for the same price by going into the used car market. What Ford did not grasp was that in the growing affluence of American society—to which his own revolution in production contributed substantially—price had become only one of the determinants in consumer choice, and not necessarily the most important one.

➤ In the mid-1920's Ford lost his ascendancy to General Motors. The latter, founded in 1908 by William C. Durant, had been handicapped at first by haphazard management and financial troubles. However, when Alfred P. Sloan, Jr. became its president in 1923, General Motors was thoroughly and systematically reorganized, with clearly defined lines of authority and responsibility. The Ford Motor Company, on the other hand, was a monolithic structure, controlled by one man who discouraged initiative on the part of subordinates. The able lieutenants who had contributed greatly to the company's success—Couzens, Wills, Knudsen—had left. Knudsen went to General Motors to become head of the Chevrolet Division and terminate the long Ford domination of the market for low-priced cars.

Henry Ford, a little too late, admitted his mistake and stopped production of the Model T on May 31, 1927, the last "flivver" to roll off the assembly line being No. 15,007,003. It took about eighteen months to put a replacement into production and in the interval another competitor, Chrysler, secured a foothold in the low-priced market with the Plymouth. Only Henry Ford could have survived this performance, and the fact that he did is a striking illustration of his grasp on the popular imagination. People took it for granted that a new automotive miracle was in the making. Dealers kept their franchises and waited patiently for a new car to sell. When the Model A Ford finally appeared, customers were lined up at the showrooms. The success was temporary; Chevrolet recovered its leadership after a year, and Ford had to remain content with second place.

The last phase of Henry Ford's career saw him facing conditions that he neither understood nor liked. He had never been flexible in his ideas, and he was unable to accept the changes brought about by the Depression and the New Deal. He was an elderly man by this time, and his health was beginning to fail. During this period he came under the influence of Harry Bennett, who appears to have made his way into Ford's confidence by playing on his fears for the safety of the Ford grandsons (following the kidnapping and murder of the son of Charles A. Lindbergh). Bennett became head of the Ford Security Department and from this post interfered in every phase of the company's operations, besides fomenting friction between Henry Ford and his son Edsel.

When the New Deal administration came into power, one of its first major steps was to try to promote industrial recovery through the National Industry Recovery Act, which called for codes of fair competition in each industry, including acceptance of collective bargaining for labor. The program was usually referred to as NRA, for the National Recovery Administration, the agency charged with applying it. The rest of the automobile industry duly complied, without overwhelming enthusiasm, and formulated a code, but Ford refused to accept it. Part of the reason was that he was not going to have the government tell him how to run his business; part was his maverick personality. He was not an organization man; the Ford Motor Company was never in his lifetime a member of any of the automobile industry's trade associations and did not subscribe to the agreement for cross-licensing of patents arranged after the Selden suit— although Ford went along with the system in practice.

Even in decline the spell of the Ford name remained powerful, so much so that the government backed away from a showdown. Ford could claim that he did not need to sign the automobile code because his wage and hour standards were better than the code required, but he was still technically in violation of the law. Nevertheless the government did not prosecute him and only half-heartedly invoked its own regulations prohibiting the purchase of goods from companies that did not comply with the codes. Evidently the Roosevelt administration, popular and powerful as it was, hesitated to challenge Henry Ford.

The growing power of labor during the New Deal proved to be a more formidable problem than the constitutionally weak NRA. The whole automobile industry resisted unionization for some time, but after Franklin D. Roosevelt's one-sided victory in the 1936 election and the Supreme Court's decision the following spring sustaining the constitutionality of the Wagner Act, all the automobile firms except Ford bowed to the inevitable with as good grace as possible. General Motors led the way by coming to terms with the United Automobile Workers in 1937. Ford insisted that his men were loyal to the company and had no wish to be organized. He undoubtedly believed it, but by now he was out of touch with the men who worked for him. He heard only what Bennett chose to tell him about labor conditions. The result was bad publicity for the Ford Motor Company: for example, the "battle of the overpass" on May 26, 1937, when Walter Reuther and other UAW organizers were attacked without provocation and beaten by some of Bennett's men. When, four years later, a spectacular strike demonstrated convincingly that his workers did want to organize, it was a bitter disillusionment for Henry Ford.

Ford's nonbusiness interests and activities changed in character as he grew older. To the end of his life Henry Ford was prepared to make positive pronouncements on any subject that came to his attention, but his desire for political office died with his presidential aspirations. He engaged in some philanthropy, largely under the influence of Mrs. Ford. The Henry Ford Hospital in Detroit was one conspicuous result. The Ford Foundation originated in 1936, but at that time it was primarily a device to avoid estate taxes that would inevitably have cost the Ford heirs control of the company. Its rise as one of the major philanthropic foundations occurred after Henry Ford's death.

He also developed antiquarian interests, founding the Ford Museum and Greenfield Village to preserve artifacts of the American past, and even trying to revive folk dancing. As is suggested later, this activity was to some extent undertaken to remove the stigma of the "History is bunk" legend; it also reflects a nostalgia for the simple rural society of his youth.

Henry Ford was a family man, but he failed tragically in his relations with his only son, Edsel. Ford wanted Edsel to be a replica of himself, and Edsel, in effect, never had a chance to lead his own life. Henry Ford attached little value to formal education, so Edsel was not permitted to go to college; Edsel became president of the Ford Motor Company in 1920, but his father continued to dictate policy; and in the 1930's Edsel was subjected to constant interference and harassment by Harry Bennett. Edsel died in 1943 from undulant fever and stomach ulcers that turned to cancer, undoubtedly aggravated by the constant frustrations under which he had to live and work.

By this time Henry Ford's sun had definitely set. A severe stroke in 1938 began a physical decline, but he stubbornly retained his one-man control of his company, working through Bennett in such a way that it was never quite clear who was actually issuing the orders. When World War II came, Ford at first repeated the isolationist pacifism of his earlier years and then made grandiose pronouncements about what he could do in military production: a thousand airplanes of standard design a day, for example. The result was that his company's quite considerable contributions to the war effort were undervalued because they did not fulfill the extravagant expectations that had been aroused. The new Ford-operated aircraft factory at Willow Run, Michigan, was so slow in getting started that it was sardonically termed "Will-It Run?"

When Edsel died it was clear that his father could no longer manage the Ford Motor Company if the company was to survive. Edsel's oldest son, Henry Ford II, was brought back from the Navy to take charge. With this event the elder Ford effectively passed into history, although his death did not occur until April 7, 1947.

Chronology of the Life of Henry Ford

1863	(July 30) Born, Wayne County, Michigan, near Dearborn, son of William and Mary Litogot Ford.
1879	Leaves home to become apprentice in Detroit. George B. Selden applies for patent on "road engine."
1882	Returns to Dearborn.
1888	Marries Clara Bryant.
1891	Goes to work for Detroit Illuminating Company.
1893	Edsel Ford born. Duryea car run in Springfield, Massachusetts; first American gasoline automobile.
1895	Selden patent issued.
1896	(June 4) First Ford car, the quadricycle, run in Detroit.
1899	Becomes superintendent of Detroit Automobile Company.
1900	Detroit Automobile Company replaced by Henry Ford Company.
1901–2	Builds and drives racing cars.
1903	Ford Motor Company organized. Selden patent suit against Ford begun.
1908	Model T introduced.
1909	Selden patent sustained in district court.
1910	Highland Park plant goes into operation.
1911	Circuit Court of Appeals rules Selden patent "valid but not infringed."
1913	Introduces moving assembly-line production.
1914	Ford Motor Company announces five dollars a day basic wage.
1915	Sails on "peace ship" expedition.
1916	Dodge brothers sue Ford for payment of dividends. Work on River Rouge plant begun.
1918	Runs unsuccessfully for United States Senator from Michigan.
1919	Loses Dodge suit. Becomes publisher of *Dearborn Independent*. Wins nominal verdict in libel suit against *Chicago Tribune*. Edsel Ford becomes president of Ford Motor Company.
1920	Anti-Semitic campaign begun in *Dearborn Independent*.
1921	Surmounts major financial crisis during 1920-21 depression.

1922	Acquires Lincoln Motor Company.
1925	Acquires Stout Metal Airplane Company and begins building Ford trimotors.
1927	Model T discontinued.
1928	Model A introduced.
1932	V-8 introduced. Airplane manufacture discontinued.
1933	Defies NRA; refuses to sign automobile code. Greenfield Village opened.
1936	Ford Foundation created.
1937	Conflict with UAW; union organizers attacked outside River Rouge plant ("Battle of the Overpass").
1941	UAW wins strike against Ford. Willow Run bomber plant begun.
1943	Death of Edsel Ford. Henry Ford II becomes president of Ford Motor Company.
1947	(April 7) Dies, Dearborn, Michigan.

FORD SPEAKS TO THE WORLD

Henry Ford expressed his opinions freely but seldom directly. Most of what appeared under his name was filtered through secretaries, editors, and public relations men. But he did take the stand in three important lawsuits, and on these occasions it may be assumed that, however carefully his lawyers coached him, his responses were authentic. The books cited here are collections of Ford's ideas. Two were written by Samuel Crowther and the third is a series of interviews by F. L. Faurote. The language is Crowther's and Faurote's, but the ideas expressed are Ford's.

1
√ The Early Steps

These selections from Henry Ford's testimony in the Selden patent case give his own account of his first experiments with motor vehicles. His description of the development of mechanical interests in his boyhood is certainly authentic, but the chronology given for his first car leaves something to be desired. His lawyers undoubtedly wanted to establish—if it were at all possible to do so—that Ford had built a functioning car before the Selden patent was issued in 1895, and he probably was experimenting with the idea at the time he states. However, there is no acceptable evidence that he had a vehicle operating on the streets of Detroit before 1896, and the car that he sold to Mr. Charles Ainsley was the 1896 quadricycle. The dates claimed by Ford would put his car ahead of the Duryea car of 1893 as the first practical American gasoline automobile, and it is quite possible that this was Ford's purpose. The direct questioning at this particular session was done by Ford's attorney, Ralzemond A. Parker; the cross-examination by W. R. Vaill, who was one of the counsels for the prosecution.

THE FIRST FORDS [1]

July 20, 1904

I made a small gas engine in this experimental shop. In 1890 I started to make a double cylinder gas engine for an automobile—I completed the engine in the winter of 1891 and 1892.

Q. 56   How do you fix that date?
A.   Because it was the first year I started with the Edison Light Co.
Q. 57   What became of that machine that you say you completed in the winter of 1891 or 92?
A.   I ran it around for two or three years; and I sold it to Mr. C. Ainsley of Detroit; and he sold it to other parties, and I bought it back last winter.

July 21

Q. 66   In your answer to question 57, you said you ran it around two or three years; what years were those?
A.   1893, 94, and 95.
Q. 67   Where was it run?
A.   In Detroit.
Q. 69   Was it on the highway, streets?
A.   Yes, on the streets.
Q. 70   What can you say as to whether or not the general public at that time had an opportunity of seeing it?
A.   Well, there were thousands saw it.
Q. 73   Have you any idea about how many miles it ran while you had it?
A.   Perhaps about one thousand.

*   *   *

Q. 177 Did you build any automobiles other than this first vehicle, and if so, when did you begin your construction of the second?
A.   Right after I sold this one.
Q. 178 Do you know when the second automobile was completed?
A.   Some time in 1897.
Q. 179 Are you now engaged in manufacturing automobiles?
A.   Yes, sir.
Q. 179a How do they compare with the first one you manufactured?
A.   Similar in the principles, have the same kind of a motor.

[1] From U. S. Circuit Court of Appeals for the Second Circuit. Columbia Motor Car Co. and G. B. Selden v. C. A. Duerr and Co. and Ford Motor Co. Transcript of Record, Appeal from Circuit Court of the U. S. for the Southern District of New York Defendant's Testimony, IX, 34–35, 872–75, 879–80, 882, 883–84.

Q. 180   Do you know what kind of a motor is generally used in gasolene auto-mobiles?

A.   Four-cycle type.

Q. 181   What can you say as to whether or not motors of this type are motors in which explosions take place?

A.   Explosions do take place in this type of motors.

Q. 182   Have you had any experience with motors employing wire gauze screens, which screens are interposed between the chamber where the explosions take place and another chamber containing an explosive mixture?

A.   No experience.

Q. 183   Did you ever see a motor in which explosions take place in which a wire gauze screen was so employed?

A.   No.

Direct-examination closed.

Cross-Examination by Mr. Vaill:

XQ. 184   The copy of the Selden patent which you have looked at states that the application was filed May 8, 1879; how old were you at that date?

A.   I was 16 years old.

XQ. 185   What experience had you in mechanical matters prior to 1880?

A.   My people say I was trying to build an automobile when I was ten years old.

Answer objected to as hearsay.

XQ. 186   When did you first have any experience of any kind with gas engines or engines operated by gas or gasolene?

A.   Nothing with gasolene until about 1890 or 1891.

XQ. 187   Had you ever had any previous experience with engines which used a previously made gas, not made from gasolene, immediately before its use in the engine?

A.   Not very much.

XQ. 188   Please state how much.

A.   I saw them running in Detroit about 1883, or 1884; did some repairing on them at the Eagle Iron Works in 1884.

XQ. 189   What type of engines were those referred to in your last answer?

A.   The Otto type.*

XQ. 190   What particular parts of those engines were you called upon to repair?

A.   Fitting the slide valves in the valves.

XQ. 191   After this experience with the Otto engines referred to, what was the first work you did on your own account in connection with gas or gasolene engines?

A.   Was, in about 1887 or 1888, in a small repair shop of my own.

XQ. 192   Did you complete and actually operate the engines worked on in your repair shop, and if so, what was the date of such completion and opera-tion?

---

* [Introduced by A. N. Otto in Germany in 1876, this was the first successful four-cycle internal combustion engine—ed.]

A.   No, I did not complete any machines.

XQ. 193 Why did you not complete the experimental engine?

A.   Mine was mostly repair work and belonged to other people.

XQ. 194 When did you first complete and operate a gasolene engine?

A.   About 1890.

XQ. 195 What type of engine was that?

A.   Otto type, experimental engine.

XQ. 196 This was a stationary engine, was it not?

A.   Yes.

XQ. 197 What became of this engine?

A.   It was destroyed.

XQ. 198 Accidentally or intentionally?

A.   Likely gave it to somebody.

XQ. 199 Do you mean you gave it to somebody for old iron?

A.   No.

XQ. 200 For what reasons did you give it away?

A.   Because a young man wanted it, I think.

XQ. 201 Was it operative at the time you gave it away?

A.   It was.

XQ. 202 How many horsepower was this engine that you gave away?

A.   It was a small engine, about an inch bore by three stroke.

XQ. 203 Do you know whether or not it was destroyed after you gave it away?

A.   I think it was.

XQ. 204 What is the first gasolene operated engine that you have preserved?

A.   The one in this small motor carriage.

XQ. 205 Do you mean the one on the automobile that you have referred to in connection with the exhibits shown you this morning?

A.   Yes.

*   *   *

XQ. 250 Is it not true as a general proposition that all American automobiles propelled by gasolene in a motor of the explosive type are practically the same in the essential features?

A.   Yes.

XQ. 251 How is comparing American automobiles with European or foreign machines?

A.   The same.

XQ. 252 What are the greatest differences among American machines that you have noticed up to the present time?

A.   In the weight of the machine.

XQ. 253 Is this about all the difference you can think up?

A.   Yes.

XQ. 254 If you have ever taken out any patents on automobiles or parts of the same what features do these patents relate to as a general thing?

A.   The driving mechanism and transmission.

XQ. 255 That is, you mean different devices for connecting the engine with the driving axle or wheels, is that correct?

A.   Yes.

XQ. 256   Have you ever taken out any patents for any particular way of mounting the engine on the vehicle?

A.   No.

XQ. 257   Are the devices which you have patented embodied in the machines as are at present manufactured by the Ford Motor Company?

A.   Yes.

XQ. 258   Have the devices of these patents been copied to any great extent so as to warrant the bringing of suits for infringement?

A.   — [No answer to this question is given in the transcript—ed.]

XQ. 259   Outside of your own experiments with gasolene engines from what have you obtained your knowledge of the subject?

A.   By reading and experience.

XQ. 260   Reading what?

A.   All subjects on automobiles.

XQ. 261   Please name some of the books or pamphlets most prominent (*sic*) connected with this subject and from which you have obtained information?

A.   American Machinist and Horseless Age.

XQ. 262   What was the first gas engine that gave you the first definite idea as to its principle and operation?

A.   Otto gas engine.

XQ. 263   What time was this and where did you first obtain knowledge of the Otto engine?

A.   About 1880, in Detroit and also from English Scientific books, that I had in 1879.

*   *   *

XQ. 279   What different kinds of work did you do while located with the Edison Lighting Company for the eight years subsequent to 1890?

A.   Mechanical engineer, had charge of all the machinery.

XQ. 280   Did you do the repairing yourself or merely direct others?

A.   Some of it and directed others.

XQ. 281   Your work there had nothing to do with designing the construction of automobiles, had it?

A.   I had an experimental room in which I worked nights.

XQ. 282   Is this the same experimental shop you have referred to before.

A.   No.

XQ. 283   Then in this shop you experimented with gasolene engines for automobiles, did you?

A.   Yes.

XQ. 284   How much did you work in this shop during the whole period you were with the Edison Illuminating Company?

A.   Whenever I had any spare time.

XQ. 285   How much did that amount to in a week or month?

A.   Evenings and all night Saturday night.

XQ. 286   Did you complete any machines or automobiles while you were with the Edison Illuminating Company?

A.   Yes.

XQ. 287 How many?

A.   Two.

XQ. 288 Are they still in existence?

A.   Yes.

*   *   *

XQ. 295 If the Selden patent in suit is sustained as valid and infringed, either in the present suit or that against the Ford Motor Company and injunction should issue against the Ford Motor Company, do you consider that it would be detrimental to your business?

Objected to as indefinite.

A.   No.

XQ. 296 You had rather see the Selden patent declared invalid than sustained, would you not?

A.   It would not effect us, as we do not infringe the Selden patent, in my mind.

The latter part of the answer is objected to as volunteered.

XQ. 297 Aside from your opinion of the question of infringement you had rather see the patent in suit invalidated than sustained, would you not?

A.   I don't think it makes any difference to me. In fact, I would rather see it sustained.

XQ. 298 Then you consider the Selden patent a benefit to your business, do you not?

Objected to as immaterial.

A.   It does not make any difference, as I don't think we infringe it.

XQ. 299 Do you think the Selden patent has been any benefit in your business of manufacturing automobiles in the past?

Same objection.

A.   Yes, through the publicity we have obtained through fighting it.

THE CAR FOR THE GREAT MULTITUDE [2]

The following letter was signed by Henry Ford and as far as it is possible to judge was actually written by him. It appeared just as the Ford Motor Company was introducing the Model N, the immediate predecessor of the Model T, which it closely resembled. What Ford is saying represents a significant step toward the realization of his dream of "a car for the great multitude." The concept of a low-priced car for general use was by no means unique to Henry Ford. Other automotive pioneers saw the potential of the mass market and some, notably Alanson Brush and Ransom E. Olds, made determined efforts to penetrate it. However, they began by designing a car that could

[2] From *The Automobile,* XIV (January 11, 1906), 107–19

be built cheaply and consequently produced light-weight buggies that would not stand hard usage. Only Ford realized that the first requisite was to formulate the qualities that a "universal" car must possess and design the vehicle accordingly; after that the problem of low-cost production could be attacked.

Arranging to Build 20,000 Runabouts

Editor *The Automobile:*

There are more people in this country who can buy automobiles than in any other country on the face of the globe, and in the history of the automobile industry in this country the demand has never yet been filled. Some statisticians figure it that the factories of this country were only able to fill 75 per cent of the demand in the season past, and only 66-2/3 per cent of the demand in the previous season. In spite of increased facilities and a marked improvement in the construction of automobiles, the prospect of filling the demand this season is exceedingly slim, and for this reason most of the factories building cars claim that prices should be maintained and to put out a low-priced car is unjustifiable and suicidal.

The assertion has often been made that it would be only a question of a few years before the automobile industry would go the way the bicycle went. I think this is in no way a fair comparison and that the automobile, while it may have been a luxury when first put out, is now one of the absolute necessities of our later day civilization. The bicycle was a recreation and a fad. The automobile, while it is a recreation, is in no way a fad.

The greatest need today is a light, low-priced car with an up-to-date engine of ample horsepower, and built of the very best material. One that will go anywhere a car of double the horsepower will; that is in every way an automobile and not a toy; and, most important of all, one that will not be a wrecker of tires and a spoiler of the owner's disposition. It must be powerful enough for American roads and capable of carrying its passengers anywhere that a horse-drawn vehicle will go without the driver being afraid of ruining his car.

It must be a handy car, not too cumbersome, and one where a chauffeur will not be absolutely necessary either as a driver or because of his mechanical skill; a car which the owner can leave in front of his office and which will be ready to start at any time and take him wherever he wishes to go.

Motors must be water-cooled, for it is vastly more important that the working parts should be protected from the natural heat of a gas engine in this way than that a few dollars may be saved by cutting out the cost of a radiator and circulation system to the benefit only of the manufacturer's profit and loss account.

Automobiles have been built too heavy in the past. The theory that to get strength you must have thickness or density in material was long ago exploded as false. Of course, there is a danger point, and cars can be too light and without enough substance to hold together, regardless of the material used. It must have weight enough to give it good traction, and the key word for getting cars down to a rational weight is, without doubt, "Simplicity." The engines must be simplified to get them within the comprehension of the ordinary owner.

Heavy cars are expensive to run in many ways, and while expense is no item worthy of notice to some owners in this country, the lack of patience to bother with a muddy, cranky, unwieldy rubber tire is certainly universal.

We are today in a position to build and deliver 10,000 of our four-cylinder runabouts. I am now making arrangements whereby we can build and deliver 20,000 of these runabouts, and all within twelve months.

Ford Motor Company,
Detroit, Michigan   Henry Ford

2

On Business

On November 2, 1916, John and Horace Dodge brought a minority stockholders' suit to compel Henry Ford to distribute three-fourths of the Ford Motor Company's cash surplus as dividends, a step which threatened Ford's plans for expansion, including the building of a giant new plant on the River Rouge. The specific details of the complaint are included as an introduction to Ford's testimony, but there were larger issues. The fundamental one was how large corporate earnings should be allocated among the claims of stockholders, wage increases, price reduction, and plant expansion. The case consequently permitted, indeed required Ford to describe his philosophy of business.

There were supplementary factors. Ford was annoyed because he felt that the Dodges were using their share of his profits to produce a competing car—as they were. There were also questions of the powers of the Ford Motor Company under its charter and of whether the disputed decisions had been properly submitted to the board of directors and the stockholders.

The decision went against Ford, with the result that he decided that he would not again be subjected to this kind of restraint. In 1919 he bought out all his stockholders, so that all the stock in the company was held by the Ford family.

In the first part of this selection Ford was being questioned by the Dodge attorney, Elliott G. Stevenson. At the point indicated in the text, his own attorney, Alfred Lucking, took over.

"THE PRICE WAS TOO HIGH"[1]

Excerpts from Plaintiff's Complaint

11. That the said Ford Motor Company has for a number of years regularly paid, quarterly, a dividend equal to five per cent (5%) monthly

---

[1] From State of Michigan, Circuit Court of Wayne County. Transcript of testimony, John F. and Horace E. Dodge v. Ford Motor Co., Henry Ford, et al., No. 56660 (1916), pp. 6–7, 101–2, 103–4, 116, 207–9, 228–30, 243–44, 274, 275.

upon the authorized capital stock of the Company of Two million dollars ($2,000,000).

That in January, 1914, it declared and paid a special dividend of Ten million dollars ($10,000,000); in May, 1914, a special dividend of Two million dollars ($2,000,000); in June, 1914, a special dividend of Two million dollars ($2,000,000); in July, 1914, two special dividends of Two million dollars ($2,000,000) each; in October, 1914, a special dividend of Three million dollars ($3,000,000); in May, 1915, a special dividend of Ten million dollars ($10,000,000); in Ocotber, 1915, a special dividend of Five million dollars ($5,000,000).

12. That notwithstanding the enormous earnings for the fiscal year ending July 31, 1916, to wit, approximately Sixty million dollars ($60,000,000), the said Ford Motor Company has not since declared any special dividends and the said Henry Ford, President of said Company, has declared it to be the settled policy of the Company not to pay in the future any special dividends, but to put back into the business for the future all the earnings of the Company, other than the regular dividend of five per cent (5%) monthly upon the authorized capital stock of the Company—Two million dollars ($2,000,000).

13. That such declaration of the future policy of the said Henry Ford as the controlling stockholder and factor in fixing the policy for the management of said corporation was published in the public press in the City of Detroit and the public press throughout the United States in substantially the following language:

"My ambition," declared Mr. Ford, "is to employ still more men; to spread the benefits of this industrial system to the greatest possible number, to help them build up their lives and their homes. To do this, we are putting the greatest share of our profits back into the business."

14. That the said Henry Ford has stated directly to your orators personally, in substance, that as all of the stockholders of the Company had received back in dividends more than they had invested, that they were not entitled to receive anything additional to the regular dividend of five per cent (5%) per month and that it was not his policy to have larger dividends declared in the future and that the profits and earnings of the Company would be put back into the business for the purpose of extending its operations and increasing the number of its employees and that inasmuch as the profits are to be represented by investment in plants and capital investment, the stockholders would have no right to complain.

15. That while the said regular dividend of five per cent (5%) per month—60% per annum—on the authorized capital stock of the Company—$2,000,000—seems large, considered separate and apart from the accumulated surplus of the Company, yet when such surplus is taken into account, such dividend amounts to but a fraction over one per cent (1%)

of the capital invested in the conduct of the business of the Company and is wholly inadequate and as earnings upon such capital so invested in said corporation is unreasonably inadequate.

Ford Testimony

Q. To what extent have you considered the necessity for increased facilities for production of cars?
A. We expect to increase it double.
Q. To double; that is, you produced 500,000 cars, with the old plant, as we speak of it, as up to July 31st, 1916?
A. Yes, sir.
Q. And you are duplicating that plant, or more than duplicating it?
A. About duplicating it.
Q. Your policy is to increase the production to a million cars per annum?
A. Yes, sir.
Q. Yes. You are not satisfied with producing five hundred thousand cars per annum?
A. The demand was not satisfied.
Q. The demand was not satisfied?
A. No.
Q. Do you mean that the Ford Motor Company during the year 1915 and '16, when it produced and sold 500,000 cars, could not meet the demand?
A. *Could not* quite meet the demand; and, besides, we left the price——
Q. What is that?
A. We left the price as it was the preceding car [*sic*].
Q. That is, you left the price in 1915 and '16 the same as the year 1913 and '14?
A. Left the price the same in 1916.
Q. What?
A. We left the price the same in 1916 as we did in 1915.
Q. Your fiscal year ends July 31st, 1916?
A. Yes, sir.
Q. So that year would include from July 31st, 1915, to July 31st, 1916?
A. Yes, sir.
Q. And you left the price of the car——
A. Yes, sir.
Q. The same for 1915–16 as for 1914–15?
A. *Yes; for the purpose of accumulating money* to make these extensions.
Q. You *found* that even with the old price, and the increased production to 500,000 cars a year, you were unable to keep up with the demand for the car?
A. *Just about.*
Q. *Just about?*
A. *Yes.*
Q. So far as your experience of 1915 and '16 was concerned, you had good reason to believe that you could duplicate that production and sell it at the same price during the next year, didn't you?
A. *Yes, but that isn't our policy.*

Q. Well, that is, you are satisfied you could do that?
A. No, we couldn't do it.
Q. What is that?
A. No, we couldn't do it; not keep the same price.
Q. Not, and produce the same number of cars?
A. Not and keep the same price.
Q. Why not?
A. Because the price was too high.
Q. Well, you could not meet the demand the year before, you say?
A. That has been always our policy, to reduce the price.
Q. You said, in answer to my question, that you produced 500,000 cars, and that they did not meet the demand; was that true, or wasn't it?
A. When?
Q. For the year 1915 and '16?
A. I don't know as to '15 and 16; I don't know anything about it.
Q. The year ending the 31st of July, 1916; that is the end of your fiscal year, is it?
A. Yes, sir.
Q. I mean the year preceding that?
A. The year preceding that?
Q. Yes, the year that this financial statement that we have referred to, covered and represented.
A. 1916 was the financial statement.
Q. Do you call that the 1916 business?
A. Yes.
Q. We will call it the 1916 business; then, for the year of 1916, you produced 500,000 cars, and you sold them?
A. Yes, sir.
Q. And you said that didn't meet the demand, those 500,000 cars?
A. Not quite.
Q. Not quite; so that you had no reason to believe, from the experience of 1916, that you could not sell 500,000 more cars in 1917?
A. No.
Q. At the same price, had you?
A. Yes, sir, we did.
Q. What reason did you have?
A. The price was too high.
Q. Why was the price too high, if you were able to sell them?
A. Because we looked ahead to know what we could sell the next year.
Q. How could you know what you could sell the next year?
A. Just from the way we run our business.
Q. Tell us that secret, how you judge, when you were able to do it in 1916, you were not able to meet the demand, that you could not do it the next year?
A. The only thing that makes anything not sell is because the price is too high.

*   *   *

Q. You say you do not think it is right to make so much profits? What is this business being continued for, and why is it being enlarged?

A. To do as much as possible for everybody concerned.

Q. What do you mean by "doing as much good as possible"?

A. To make money and use it, give employment, and send out the car where the people can use it.

Q. Is that all? Haven't you said that you had money enough yourself, and you were going to run the Ford Motor Company thereafter to employ just as many people as you could, to give them the benefits of the high wages that you paid, and to give the public the benefit of a low priced car?

A. I suppose I have, and incidentally make money.

Q. Incidentally make money?

A. Yes, sir.

Q. But your controlling feature, so far as your policy, since you have got all the money you want, is to employ a great army of men at high wages, to reduce the selling price of your car, so that a lot of people can buy it at a cheap price, and give everybody a car that wants one?

A. If you give all that, the money will fall into your hands; you can't get out of it.

*   *   *

Q. You don't have very much regard for stockholders, anyway, do you?

A. I have shown quite a regard.

Q. You have?

A. I have paid them lots of dividends.

Q. You have called them parasites, on occasions, haven't you?

A. Not Mr. Dodge, no, sir; not Dodge Brothers; I learned that word from Mr. Dodge.

Q. You learned that from Dodge?

A. Yes. He called all people that did not work, parasites.

Q. You called your stockholders parasites?

A. No, I did not.

Q. But you didn't mean Mr. Dodge?

A. No, never.

Q. Who did you refer to?

    MR. LUCKING: I object to that as an unnecessary bit of dirt.

Q. I purpose to show that this man has absolutely shown incapacity to appreciate his relation to the stockholders of this corporation.

A. Do you claim that I called the stockholders parasites?

Q. Yes, I do, in a published statement.

A. A published statement?

Q. What? Do you say that you did not?

A. I may have been quoted.

Q. Do you say that you did not?

A. I never have called anyone a parasite.

Q. "Ford is building his tractor plant on Dearborn site. Will use building where 'gasoline horse' was designed. Two other structures to form nucleus of works. Employees to share profits; no stockholders or parasites."

A. I told that man not to put that word in, parasites.

Q. You told him not to?
A. Yes, sir.
Q. You used the word, and then told him not to put it in?
A. He used it.
Q. But didn't you use it first?
A. No, I didn't use it; I told him not to put it in. He wrote the article.
Q. And you told him not to put the word "parasites," in?
A. Yes.
Q. "The old Wagner brickyard in the southeast corner of the village, is the site of the tractor plant which is already under way, with several score of workmen busy on buildings. The first of two new buildings is completed, and the other is progressing rapidly. Will be no 'parasites.' With the announcement Friday of the beginning at Dearborn, Mr. Ford gave the following outline of the directing force behind the project: 'In the new tractor plant there will be no stockholders, no directors, no absentee owners, no parasites,' he said."
A. Well, I told him not to use the word "parasites."
Q. Didn't you use those words?
A. No, sir.
Q. You didn't use those words?
A. No sir; I never used them.
Q. Why did you tell him not to use them, if you didn't use them?
A. Because he put them in, and I didn't want him to use it.
Q. Where did he put it in?
A. He put it in the article, that he was preparing.
Q. He submitted the article that he prepared, to you, did he?
A. Yes.
Q. And you told him not to use "parasites"?
A. Yes.

*   *   *

Cross-Examination by Alfred Lucking

Q. Was your action in reducing the price this year any different from what you have done many times before?
A. No, sir.
Q. What has been the uniform result up to this time?
A. Well, we have always made lots of money.
Q. What is that?
A. We have always made lots of money out of it.
Q. How long ago was it that you were making about 25,000 cars a year?
A. Five or six years, I guess. Somewheres about eight or nine years, I guess.
Q. This is 1916?
A. Yes. I think we made 18,000 in 1906.
Q. When you were making 25,000 a year, what was your next proposed jump in amount?
A. I think 75,000.
Q. Who was it that proposed that?

A. I did.
Q. Was it opposed?
A. Yes, I guess it was opposed.
Q. Was there any institution in the world making 25,000 cars, except yourselves, at that time?
A. I don't think so.
Q. You proposed to jump to 75,000?
A. Yes.
Q. The wise heads shook their heads, did they, at that time?
A. I think they did.
Q. The wise ones shook their heads?
A. The wise ones shook their heads at 10,000.
Q. How did your jump from 25,000 to 75,000 turn out?
A. Very profitably, I guess.
Q. Did the country absorb the cars?
A. Yes, sir.
Q. Bought the cars, did they?
A. Yes, sir.
Q. You reduced the price, did you?
A. Reduced the price.
Q. Who was it decided upon the policy of making a single standard article, cheap priced article?
A. I did.

*   *   *

Q. I think, in this newspaper article that Mr. Stevenson has criticized so much, you were quoted as figuring something about how much they made. Did you make that estimate, ten million dollars profit on the twenty-seven million dollars?
A. I thought perhaps they made that much.
Q. In your judgment, was that a fair statement?
A. I think it was.
Q. You didn't begrudge it to them at all, did you?
A. Not a particle.
Q. Not at all. But they made it, as near as you can tell?
A. Yes.
Q. And on their ten thousand dollars that they ventured in this way, how much in dividends have they taken out from the Ford Motor Company?
A. Why, I think about five and a half millions.
Q. Five and a half million in dollars?
A. In dollars.
Q. Cash?
A. Cash.
Q. And your regular dividends, that are paid uniformly, not as special dividends, regular dividends, are how much?
A. Sixty per cent on the capital stock, at the present time.
Q. Sixty per cent of the capital stock?

A. Yes, sir.
Q. How much of that have they got?
A. There is two million capital.
Q. They have ten per cent of it, two hundred thousand dollars?
A. Yes, sir.
Q. They have two hundred thousand dollars of the capital stock for their original ten thousand dollar investment?
A. Yes, sir.
Q. That is an increase, without putting in any additional money?
A. Yes.
Q. On that $200,000.00, your regular dividends are $120,000.00 a year, that is, sixty per cent of $200,000.00?
A. $1,200,000.00.
Q. No, but on their ten per cent.
A. Yes.
Q. $120,000.00.
A. I guess so.
Q. That is twelve hundred per cent per annum, is it, on their original ten thousand dollars, they get regularly. You have paid a little more than the usual six per cent that we get on money, that most people are glad to get?
A. In special dividends, yes.
Q. Yes.
A. Yes, we do pay special dividends.
Q. You know a good many corporations in this town that, from their start-off, have never paid more than six per cent on their original capital subscribed, don't you?
A. Well, I don't know very much about it.
Q. Well, the rest of us do, unfortunately; a lot of others don't pay anything; they are getting 1,200 per cent on their original investment regularly, is that right?
A. That is right, I guess.

"A REASONABLE PROFIT—BUT NOT TOO MUCH" [2]

Bear in mind; every time you reduce the price of the car without reducing the quality, you increase the possible number of purchasers. There are many men who will pay $360 for a car who would not pay $440. We had in round numbers 500,000 buyers of cars on the $440 basis, and I figure that on the $360 basis we can increase the sales to possibly 800,000 cars for the year—less profit on each car, but more cars, more employment of labor, and in the end we get all the total profit we ought to make.

And let me say right here, that I do not believe that we should make such an awful profit on our cars. A reasonable profit is right, but not too

[2] From an interview published in the *Detroit News*, November 4, 1916.

much. So it has been my policy to force the price of the car down as fast as production would permit, and give the benefits to users and laborers, with resulting surprisingly enormous benefits to ourselves.

The men associated with me haven't always agreed with this policy—— Dodge Brothers say I ought to continue to ask $440 for a car. I don't believe in such awful profits. I don't believe it is right.

So, would I be serving the interests of our firm best by holding up the price because the manufacturer of another automobile wants us to, or by reducing the price in the interest of our own customers, our own employes, and our own business standing, and profit? I think I am right in my policy.

Further ideas on the conduct of business appear in excerpts from the two books written for Ford by Samuel Crowther. It is ironic that in an era when the ghost writer has become commonplace, Henry Ford continues to be criticized for having his ideas expressed by a professional journalist. As stated previously, the ideas are Ford's own, and the collaboration was publicly acknowledged.

There is a distinction between the two books. My Life and Work *appeared when Ford was at his zenith and the boom period of the 1920's was developing.* Moving Forward *was published in 1930, when the whole economy was visibly declining and the Ford Motor Company no longer dominated the automotive world. In the first book Ford could speak with complete self-confidence; in the second he was plainly on the defensive.*

BUSINESS VERSUS FINANCE [3]

The automobile business was not on what I would call an honest basis, to say nothing of being, from a manufacturing standpoint, on a scientific basis, but it was no worse than business in general. That was the period, it may be remembered, in which many corporations were being floated and financed. The bankers, who before then had confined themselves to the railroads, got into industry. My idea was then and still is that if a man did his work well, the price he would get for that work, the profits and all financial matters, would care for themselves and that a business ought to start small and build itself up and out of its earnings. If there are no earnings then that is a signal to the owner that he is wasting his time and does not belong in that business. I have never found it necessary to change those ideas, but I discovered that this simple formula of doing good work and getting paid for it was supposed to be slow for modern business. The plan at that time most in favour was to start off with the

[3] From Henry Ford, in collaboration with Samuel Crowther, *My Life and Work* (Garden City: Doubleday & Company, Inc., 1923), pp. 38–42. Reprinted by permission of Mrs. Mary Owens Crowther.

largest possible capitalization and then sell all the stock and all the bonds that could be sold. Whatever money happened to be left over after all the stock and bond-selling expenses and promoters charges and all that, went grudgingly into the foundation of the business. A good business was not one that did good work and earned a fair profit. A good business was one that would give the opportunity for the floating of a large amount of stocks and bonds at high prices. It was the stocks and bonds, not the work, that mattered. I could not see how a new business or an old business could be expected to be able to charge into its product a great big bond interest and then sell the product at a fair price. I have never been able to see that.

I have never been able to understand on what theory the original investment of money can be charged against a business. Those men in business who call themselves financiers say that money is "worth" 6 per cent or 5 per cent or some other per cent, and that if a business has one hundred thousand dollars invested in it, the man who made the investment is entitled to charge an interest payment on the money, because, if instead of putting that money into the business he had put it into a savings bank or into certain securities, he could have a certain fixed return. Therefore they say that a proper charge against the operating expenses of a business is the interest on this money. This idea is at the root of many business failures and most service failures. Money is not worth a particular amount. As money it is not worth anything, for it will do nothing of itself. The only use of money is to buy tools to work with or the product of tools. Therefore money is worth what it will help you to produce or buy and no more. If a man thinks that his money will earn 5 per cent or 6 per cent he ought to place it where he can get that return, but money placed in a business is not a charge on the business—or, rather, should not be. It ceases to be money and becomes, or should become, an engine of production, and it is therefore worth what it produces—and not a fixed sum according to some scale that has no bearing upon the particular business in which the money has been placed. Any return should come after it has produced, not before.

Business men believed that you could do anything by "financing" it. If it did not go through on the first financing then the idea was to "refinance." The process of "refinancing" was simply the game of sending good money after bad. In the majority of cases the need of refinancing arises from bad management, and the effect of refinancing is simply to pay the poor managers to keep up their bad management a little longer. It is merely a postponement of the day of judgment. This makeshift of refinancing is a device of speculative financiers. Their money is no good to them unless they can connect it up with a place where real work is being done, and that they cannot do unless, somehow, that place is poorly managed. Thus, the speculative financiers delude themselves that they are putting their money out to use. They are not; they are putting it out to waste.

I determined absolutely that never would I join a company in which finance came before the work or in which bankers or financiers had a part. And further that, if there were no way to get started in the kind of business that I thought could be managed in the interest of the public, then I simply would not get started at all. For my own short experience, together with what I saw going on around me, was quite enough proof that business as a mere money-making game was not worth giving much thought to and was distinctly no place for a man who wanted to accomplish anything. Also it did not seem to me to be the way to make money. I have yet to have it demonstrated that it is the way. For the only foundation of real business is service.

A manufacturer is not through with his customer when a sale is completed. He has then only started with his customer. In the case of an automobile the sale of the machine is only something in the nature of an introduction. If the machine does not give service, then it is better for the manufacturer if he never had the introduction, for he will have the worst of all advertisements—a dissatisfied customer. There was something more than a tendency in the early days of the automobile to regard the selling of a machine as the real accomplishment and that thereafter it did not matter what happened to the buyer. That is the shortsighted salesman-on-commission attitude. If a salesman is paid only for what he sells, it is not to be expected that he is going to exert any great effort on a customer out of whom no more commission is to be made. And it is right on this point that we later made the largest selling argument for the Ford. The price and the quality of the car would undoubtedly have made a market, and a large market. We went beyond that. A man who bought one of our cars was in my opinion entitled to continuous use of that car, and therefore if he had a breakdown of any kind it was our duty to see that his machine was put into shape again at the earliest possible moment. In the success of the Ford car the early provision of service was an outstanding element. Most of the expensive cars of that period were ill provided with service stations. If your car broke down you had to depend on the local repair man—when you were entitled to depend upon the manufacturer. If the local repair man were a forehanded sort of a person, keeping on hand a good stock of parts (although on many of the cars the parts were not interchangeable), the owner was lucky. But if the repair man were a shiftless person, with an inadequate knowledge of automobiles and an inordinate desire to make a good thing out of every car that came into his place for repairs, then even a slight breakdown meant weeks of laying up and a whopping big repair bill that had to be paid before the car could be taken away. The repair men were for a time the largest menace to the automobile industry. Even as late as 1910 and 1911 the owner of an automobile was regarded as essentially a rich man whose money ought to be taken away from him. We met that situation squarely and at the very beginning. We would not have our distribution blocked by stupid, greedy men.

That is getting some years ahead of the story, but it is control by finance that breaks up service because it looks to the immediate dollar. If the first consideration is to earn a certain amount of money, then, unless by some stroke of luck matters are going especially well and there is a surplus over for service so that the operating men may have a chance, future business has to be sacrificed for the dollar of to-day.

MARKETS, PRICES, AND MASS PRODUCTION [4]

No one has yet been born who can manage both to manipulate the market for its stock and also to do business in such a way that it will be profitable. The two do not and cannot mix. We have acutely brought home to us what it means to have a considerable portion of the country take its mind off doing business and engage in a career of speculating in stocks.

The immediate cure for depression, and by depression I mean a period when men are out of work and not able to improve their standards of living, is told in one word, "quantity"—quantities of goods pushed out into the world.

But it is not enough simply to manufacture goods. There is a great deal more to the process than that. There is no service in simply setting up a machine or a plant and letting it turn out goods. The service extends into every detail of the design, the making, the wages paid, and the selling price. None of these can ever be taken as right—they can only represent the best efforts of the moment. That is why quantity production demands so much more leadership than did the old production. Anyone who sets up a big plant to manufacture a product and then takes for granted that no further changes in design or materials or methods of making are necessary will in a curiously short space of time discover an overproduction and then the owners will start talking about the market being saturated.

A market is never saturated with a good product, but it is very quickly saturated with a bad one, and no matter how good anything may be when it is first produced it will not remain good unless its standard is constantly improved. This does not mean that new and startling changes should be made every little while, for that is not possible in a product

[4] From Henry Ford, in collaboration with Samuel Crowther, *Moving Forward* (Garden City: Doubleday & Company, Inc., 1930), pp. 7–9, 27–29. Reprinted by permission of Mrs. Mary Owens Crowther.

that began by being as good as it could be made. It is not necessarily good business to announce every change. The good will of the public is secured by quietly pressing for changes which will keep the product constantly more satisfactory, for then the reputation of the commodity will be simply that it always meets the buyer's needs. The public rarely asks for changes. But the public itself unconsciously changes, and a uniformly satisfactory article is one made by a management that is always pressing to improve it.

The right sales price is always the lowest price at which, all things considered, the article can be manufactured, and since experience in making and volume of sales will bring about lower costs, the sales price can as a rule constantly be lowered. It is the duty of a manufacturer constantly to lower prices and increase wages. The duty is not only to the public. A manufacturer owes this procedure to himself, for not otherwise can he control his business. There seems to be a good deal of misunderstanding on this point.

Lowering a price will generally increase business, if it is not a defensive act but a progressive movement. There are a great many strata of buying power and they are not sharply separated. They seem to vary almost from day to day, and even a slight change of price may take one into a new buying territory that has never before been explored. The reduction in price may not always be in dollars. It may be in added quality—that is, in giving more for the money. The very best reductions are those which comprehend both price and quality. A price reduction which is gained by reducing quality is not really a price reduction at all, and the public reacts in no uncertain way. There is no quicker or surer way of destroying confidence in a business than to make a price reduction which represents the giving of less and not of more value than before.

However, the reducing of prices solely to increase sales is not a sound business policy, for then the attention may shift from manufacturing to selling. Sales are primarily the result of good manufacturing and not of persuading people to buy. There is no difference between decreasing prices in order to gain sales and maintaining prices just because people seem willing to pay them. If prices are used as baits for buyers, to be raised or lowered as the buyers feel about it, it is in effect a handing over of the control of the business to the buyers to do with as they like. That is a very real control and it is exercised in very drastic fashion. This country has seen it exercised time and again.

The policy of constantly reducing prices has really more to do with management than with sales and should be considered from the manufacturing point of view and not with primary regard to the ideas of the sales end of the business.

*   *   *

The trouble with mass production—and the phrase "mass production" is quite misleading—is that it tends to become rigid and keeps on producing regardless of the market. It has been supposed that our company was an exponent of mass production. That has never been true, and I have often explained why it was not true. We have merely made a great many automobiles using the methods which we found most economical. The product has always ruled the methods of making. This is another way of saying that the needs of the public have ruled.

Rigid machine production of the kind known as mass production quickly comes to an end, for it violates the first principle of large-scale production—which is that the makers must constantly improve the design and quality of the goods turned out. That is the inexorable law of production and it has been proved time and again. Only a few of the standard articles of twenty years ago are the standard articles of today. Why? Those earlier articles became standard only because they always met the needs of the people. They were bought because they could always be depended upon to be first-class, but they were first-class only because they were constantly improved, although possibly the improvements were seldom mentioned. But if, after the reputation of the articles had become assured, and those who had built the reputation rested, or were followed by men who were content to take the product as they found it and depend on the fine reputation, then dry rot set in and the product steadily slipped back and another product took its place. No product ever remains standard. It has to be kept standard.

It is true that mass production frequently piles up great stocks of goods which cannot be sold and this leads to the belief that mass production results in overproduction. Inflexible mass production does start to pile up goods the moment the goods cease to suit the buyer or are too high in price, but this is not the fault of the production methods. It is the fault of the managers in thinking that one design or one method can for long continue. Indeed, if mass production were what it is supposed to be, there would be some cause for alarm—but only among the mass producers. For they would lose by it. It is the large producers who constantly change methods and designs; it is the small producers who cannot change. Among the peasants of Europe or the coolies of the Far East life is standardized. For endless generations they have been doing the same things the same way. Machine production in this country has diversified our life, has given a wider choice of articles than was ever before thought possible—and also it has provided the means wherewith the people may buy them. We standardize only on essential conveniences. Standardization, instead of making for sameness, has introduced unheard-of variety into our life. It is surprising that this has not been generally perceived.

All of this involves quite a fundamental change in corporate finance.

A company must do more than keep its plant and equipment in repair. It must continually be changing them to meet changes in design, materials, and methods of making—not a single item of equipment can be regarded as permanent. Not even the site can be taken as fixed. We abandoned our Highland Park plant—which was in its day the largest automobile plant in the world—and moved to the River Rouge plant because in the new plant there could be less handling of materials and consequently a saving. We frequently scrap whole divisions of our business—and as a routine affair. And then one has to be prepared against the day when a complete change may be necessary and an entirely new plant constructed to make a new product. We have gone through all of this.

3
Labor and Wages

In his own eyes, and in the eyes of many others, Henry Ford gave to the world an entirely new concept of the role of labor in industry: to wit, that the workingman was not just one of the factors of production but was also a consumer, and that the worker should share through higher wages gains in the efficiency of production. Later in his career, however, he came under sharp criticism not only for opposition to union organization but for allegedly dehumanizing labor by a system of production in which the worker monotonously repeated a single task. Ford's views, as expressed here, reflect an awareness of this criticism and offer a defense in terms of his individualistic philosophy. They are also very revealing of his concept of organization.

FORD LABOR POLICIES; THE FUTILITY OF STRIKES [1]

Now a business, in my way of thinking, is not a machine. It is a collection of people who are brought together to do work and not to write letters to one another. It is not necessary for any one department to know what any other department is doing. If a man is doing his work he will not have time to take up any other work. It is the business of those who plan the entire work to see that all of the departments are working properly toward the same end. It is not necessary to have meetings to establish good feeling between individuals or departments. It is not necessary for people to love each other in order to work together. Too much good fellowship may indeed be a very bad thing, for it may lead to one man trying to cover up the faults of another. That is bad for both men.

When we are at work we ought to be at work. When we are at play we ought to be at play. There is no use trying to mix the two. The sole object ought to be to get the work done and to get paid for it. When the work is done, then the play can come, but not before. And so the Ford factories and enterprises have no organization, no specific duties attaching to any position, no line of succession or of authority, very few titles, and no conferences. We have only the clerical help that is absolutely required;

[1] From *My Life and Work*, pp. 92–93, 105–6, 126–29, 259–61. Reprinted by permission of Mrs. Mary Owens Crowther.

we have no elaborate records of any kind, and consequently no red tape.

We make the individual responsibility complete. The workman is absolutely responsible for his work. The straw boss is responsible for the workmen under him. The foreman is responsible for his group. The department head is responsible for the department. The general superintendent is responsible for the whole factory. Every man has to know what is going on in his sphere. I say "general superintendent." There is no such formal title. One man is in charge of the factory and has been for years. He has two men with him, who, without in any way having their duties defined, have taken particular sections of the work to themselves. With them are about half a dozen other men in the nature of assistants, but without specific duties. They have all made jobs for themselves—but there are no limits to their jobs. They just work in where they best fit. One man chases stock and shortages. Another has grabbed inspection, and so on.

This may seem haphazard, but it is not. A group of men, wholly intent upon getting work done, have no difficulty in seeing that the work is done. They do not get into trouble about the limits of authority, because they are not thinking of titles. If they had offices and all that, they would shortly be giving up their time to office work and to wondering why did they not have a better office than some other fellow.

Because there are no titles and no limits of authority, there is no question of red tape or going over a man's head. Any workman can go to anybody, and so established has become this custom, that a foreman does not get sore if a workman goes over him and directly to the head of the factory. The workman rarely ever does so, because a foreman knows as well as he knows his own name that if he has been unjust it will be very quickly found out, and he shall no longer be a foreman. One of the things that we will not tolerate is injustice of any kind. The moment a man starts to swell with authority he is discovered, and he goes out, or goes back to a machine. A large amount of labour unrest comes from the unjust exercise of authority by those in subordinate positions, and I am afraid that in far too many manufacturing institutions it is really not possible for a workman to get a square deal.

*   *   *

I have not been able to discover that repetitive labour injures a man in any way. I have been told by parlour experts that repetitive labour is soul- as well as body-destroying, but that has not been the result of our investigations. There was one case of a man who all day long did little but step on a treadle release. He thought that the motion was making him one-sided; the medical examination did not show that he had been affected but, of course, he was changed to another job that used a different set of muscles. In a few weeks he asked for his old job again. It would seem reasonable to imagine that going through the same set of motions daily for eight hours would produce an abnormal body, but we have never had a case of it. We shift men whenever they ask to be shifted and we should like regularly to change them—that would be entirely feasible if only the men would have it that way. They do not like changes which they do not themselves suggest. Some of the operations are undoubtedly monotonous—so monotonous that it seems scarcely possible that any man would care to continue long at the same job. Probably the most monotonous task in the whole factory is one in which a man picks up a gear with a steel hook, shakes it in a vat of oil, then turns it into a basket. The motion never varies. The gears come to him always in exactly the same place, he gives each one the same number of shakes, and he drops it into a basket which is always in the same place. No muscular energy is required, no intelligence is required. He does little more than wave his hands gently to and fro—the steel rod is so light. Yet the man on that job has been doing it for eight solid years. He has saved and invested his money until now he has about forty thousand dollars—and he stubbornly resists every attempt to force him into a better job!

The most thorough research has not brought out a single case of a man's mind being twisted or deadened by the work. The kind of mind that does not like repetitive work does not have to stay in it. The work in each department is classified according to its desirability and skill into Classes "A," "B," and "C," each class having anywhere from ten to thirty different operations. A man comes directly from the employment office to "Class C." As he gets better he goes into "Class B," and so on into "Class A," and out of "Class A" into tool making or some supervisory capacity. It is up to him to place himself. If he stays in production it is because he likes it.

*　　*　　*

We do not have piece work. Some of the men are paid by the day and some are paid by the hour, but in practically every case there is a required standard output below which a man is not expected to fall. Were it otherwise, neither the workman nor ourselves would know whether or not wages were being earned. There must be a fixed day's work before a real wage can be paid. Watchmen are paid for presence. Workmen are paid for work.

Having these facts in hand we announced and put into operation in January, 1914, a kind of profit-sharing plan in which the minimum wage for any class of work and under certain conditions was five dollars a day. At the same time we reduced the working day to eight hours—it had been nine—and the week to forty-eight hours. This was entirely a voluntary

act. All of our wage rates have been voluntary. It was to our way of thinking an act of social justice, and in the last analyis we did it for our own
satisfaction of mind. There is a pleasure in feeling that you have made
others happy—that you have lessened in some degree the burdens of your
fellow-men—that you have provided a margin out of which may be had
pleasure and saving. Good will is one of the few really important assets
of life. A determined man can win almost anything that he goes after, but
unless, in his getting, he gains good will he has not profited much.

There was, however, no charity in any way involved. That was not
generally understood. Many employers thought we were just making the
announcement because we were prosperous and wanted advertising and
they condemned us because we were upsetting standards—violating the
custom of paying a man the smallest amount he would take. There is
nothing to such standards and customs. They have to be wiped out. Some
day they will be. Otherwise, we cannot abolish poverty. We made the
change not merely because we wanted to pay higher wages and thought
we could pay them. We wanted to pay these wages so that the business
would be on a lasting foundation. We were not distributing anything—we
were building for the future. A low wage business is always insecure.

Probably few industrial announcements have created a more world-
wide comment than did this one, and hardly any one got the facts quite
right. Workmen quite generally believed that they were going to get five
dollars a day, regardless of what work they did.

The facts were somewhat different from the general impression. The
plan was to distribute profits, but instead of waiting until the profits had
been earned—to approximate them in advance and to add them, under
certain conditions, to the wages of those persons who had been in the
employ of the company for six month or more. It was classified partic-
ipation among three classes of employees:

(1) Married men living with and taking good care of their families.
(2) Single men over twenty-two years of age who are of proved thrifty habits.
(3) Young men under twenty-two years of age, and women who are the sole
support of some next of kin.

A man was first to be paid his just wages—which were then on an
average of about fifteen per cent. above the usual market wage. He was
then eligible to a certain profit. His wages plus his profit were calculated
to give a minimum daily income of five dollars. The profit-sharing rate
was divided on an hour basis and was credited to the hourly wage rate,
so as to give those receiving the lowest hourly rate the largest proportion
of profits. It was paid every two weeks with the wages. For example, a man
who received thirty-four cents an hour had a profit rate of twenty-eight

and one half cents an hour—which would give him a daily income of five dollars. A man receiving fifty-four cents an hour would have a profit rate of twenty-one cents an hour—which would give him a daily income of six dollars.

The large wage had other results. In 1914, when the first plan went into effect, we had 14,000 employees and it had been necessary to hire at the rate of about 53,000 a year in order to keep a constant force of 14,000. In 1915 we had to hire only 6,508 men and the majority of these new men were taken on because of the growth of the business. With the old turnover of labour and our present force we should have to hire at the rate of nearly 200,000 men a year—which would be pretty nearly an impossible proposition.

*   *   *

Practically nothing of importance is secured by mere demand. That is why strikes always fail—even though they may seem to succeed. A strike which brings higher wages or shorter hours and passes on the burden to the community is really unsuccessful. It only makes the industry less able to serve—and decreases the number of jobs that it can support. This is not to say that no strike is justified—it may draw attention to an evil. Men can strike with justice—that they will thereby get justice is another question. The strike for proper conditions and just rewards is justifiable. The pity is that men should be compelled to use the strike to get what is theirs by right. No American ought to be compelled to strike for his rights. He ought to receive them naturally, easily, as a matter of course. These justifiable strikes are usually the employer's fault. Some employers are not fit for their jobs. The employment of men—the direction of their energies, the arranging of their rewards in honest ratio to their production and to the prosperity of the business—is no small job. An employer may be unfit for his job, just as a man at the lathe may be unfit. Justifiable strikes are a sign that the boss needs another job—one that he can handle. The unfit employer causes more trouble than the unfit employee. You can change the latter to another more suitable job. But the former must usually be left to the law of compensation. The justified strike, then, is one that need never have been called if the employer had done his work.

There is a second kind of strike—the strike with a concealed design. In this kind of strike the workingmen are made the tools of some manipulator who seeks his own ends through them. To illustrate: Here is a great industry whose success is due to having met a public need with efficient and skillful production. It has a record for justice. Such an industry presents a great temptation to speculators. If they can only gain control of it they can reap rich benefit from all the honest effort that has been put into it. They can destroy its beneficiary wage and profit-sharing, squeeze every last dollar out of the public, the product, and the workingman, and reduce it to the plight of other business concerns which are run on low principles. The motive may be the personal greed of the speculators or they may want to change the policy of a business because its example is embarrassing to other employers who do not want to do what is right. The industry cannot be touched from within, because its men have no reason to strike. So another method is adopted. The business may keep many outside shops busy supplying it with material. If these outside shops can be tied up, then that great industry may be crippled.

So strikes are fomented in the outside industries. Every attempt is made to curtail the factory's source of supplies. If the workingmen in the outside shops knew what the game was, they would refuse to play it, but they don't know; they serve as the tools of designing capitalists without knowing it. There is one point, however, that ought to rouse the suspicions of workingmen engaged in this kind of strike. If the strike cannot get itself settled, no matter what either side offers to do, it is almost positive proof that there is a third party interested in having the strike continue. That hidden influence does not want a settlement on any terms. If such a strike is won by the strikers, is the lot of the workingman improved? After throwing the industry into the hands of outside speculators, are the workmen given any better treatment or wages?

There is a third kind of strike—the strike that is provoked by the money interests for the purpose of giving labour a bad name. The American workman has always had a reputation for sound judgment. He has not allowed himself to be led away by every shouter who promised to create the millennium out of thin air. He has had a mind of his own and has used it. He has always recognized the fundamental truth that the absence of reason was never made good by the presence of violence. In his way the American workingman has won a certain prestige with his own people and throughout the world. Public opinion has been inclined to regard with respect his opinions and desires. But there seems to be a determined effort to fasten the Bolshevik stain on American Labour by inciting it to such impossible attitudes and such wholly unheard-of actions as shall change public sentiment from respect to criticism.

EMPLOYERS AND EMPLOYEES: THE SINGLE STANDARD [2]

In my view of wages and the relation of the employer and the employee, they are not a small universe in themselves; both are part of and dependent on the larger social world. The amount of work done for society and the amount of money society may profitably pay for that

[2] From *Moving Forward*, pp. 44–45, 47–49.

work determine the industrial relation, although that in turn is determined by the quality and extent of the service which industry may render. Improvement in these relations is always possible where the will to improvement exists.

But it is necessary to get away entirely from the thought that the relation between employers and employees has in it anything of meniality. Employers and employees are to be judged by the same standard—are they efficient or are they inefficient? An employer who is not fit for his job comes under the same law as any other inefficient worker. There is nothing in his status as employer that will save him. He has responsibilities but no divine right. If he is a good man in his job he will pay good wages, just as he will make a good product. And his workmen, directed by him, will be enabled to earn good wages. It is a matter of efficiency, not philanthropy. The only pride or satisfaction either may have in it, or even gratitude, is the feeling that this is a world that yields right results to right efforts.

But the relation between employer and employee is not in the least a sentimental one, and the artificial cultivation of good feeling only tends to obscure the real objectives. An artfully arranged attempt to stimulate good feeling usually has for its purpose the concealment of some deep source of bad feeling. Good feeling arises from the situation, or not at all. The paying and receiving of money is the paying and receiving of money. If it be not earned, it cannot be paid, and it should not be paid if it could be. If it be earned, then there is no reason for the employee being grateful for being paid what is justly due, nor for the employer being self-righteously proud for paying it. This view of the relation between the employer and the employee has many consequences which flow counter to the accepted tradition.

*   *   *

If a company operates on the theory that it owes a living to those who work for it, then in the course of time it will pass out—and be unable to pay the debt it thinks it owes. Exactly the same condition will be brought about by acting on the theory that the stockholders must always have dividends. Unless the primary service be to the public, no one will be served.

This principle does not seem thoroughly to be understood and it is often difficult to apply, for sometimes its application seems harsh. It seems to imply an indifference to human beings. But, in truth, it has human welfare as its motive. The plight of the men who become temporarily unemployed in the process seems much more important to the unthinking observer than the eventually increased service to all. It is difficult to see the whole picture and to realize that the fortunes of any individual or any group are always best served when they are made part of a larger service. The individual or the group through a short-sighted view of their interests may be wholly blameless of intentionally retarding progress, yet that is the result of any preference of private before public good. The right of a man to work is a sacred right, but to preserve a job just because it is a job may seem to be kindness to an individual, but it will be at the expense of a great many others who do not appear in the picture but who are just as worthy and conscientious as he is. Such reasoning, however, seems hard, not because there is any harshness in progress itself, but only because we view progress against a background of so many fallacies. When applied to wage earners it seems hard only because of our traditional conception of master and servant and that somehow the workman is a menial dependent on his employer. Indeed many worthy people cannot comprehend any other relation and, during those periods when the men who should be leading business fail to lead and consequently work is slack, the cry "Give men jobs" arises. Everyone would recognize the absurdity of employers parading bearing signs "Give us orders." There is essentially no difference between the actual position of the employer and the employee. That is the point. If an employer gets his orders through favors and believes that because he has served certain customers for a long time this is in itself a reason for having their orders continue, he is acting on the same false principle as the employee who thinks that his having held a job establishes upon his employer the duty of always providing him with a job. It is a poor rule that will not work for both alike. Long service by either employer or employee should be a reason for continued service—for the experience gained should render their service better than that which anyone else can give. A worker should have so profited by length of service as to make himself more valuable than any man without his experience. The same applies to an employer. But the test of a company, of a workman—or anybody or anything—is solely to be found in the service rendered. And in the end I think that it will be discovered that if all of us—no matter what may at the moment be our respective situations—rid ourselves of the notion that the world or anyone else owes us a living, we shall be the better for it. The approach of dependency, whether in a man or in a corporation, is the approach of helplessness and leads to the asking of a living by favor instead of a living by merit. The corporation which goes out seeking only profits does not get far and neither does the man who goes out seeking only wages—instead of work.

There is no natural level of wages, just as there is no natural level of profits. The conception of a natural level of wages arises out of a state of society in which everything even to the smallest detail is hallowed by tradition. If the inventiveness of an industry comes to a standstill—and this happens whenever an industry gets solely in the control of the financial point of view—then there will be a level of wages and for a time there will be a level of profits. But this level will be only temporary and will steadily be lowered. Industry that has found its level will soon be out of tune with the public—which never finds a level—and will cease to render a service, and then both profits and wages will begin to diminish and finally will reach the vanishing point.

4
Economic Ideas

Henry Ford's opinions on economic matters were eagerly sought and freely expressed, but his ideas do not fall into a coherent pattern. The nearest approach to a systematic organization of his economic ideas is a collection of interviews by Fay L. Faurote, first published in The Forum *and then collected in book form as* My Philosophy of Industry. *Samples from this work show the nature of Ford's thinking on economic matters, plus some of the fads that he was constantly taking up. Faurote had a previous contact with Ford as co-author, with H. L. Arnold, of* The Ford Methods *and the Ford Shops. Excerpts from this book appear in Part Two. It also seems appropriate to include Ford's views on the economic significance of the motor vehicle.*

POWER, MONEY, AND POVERTY [1]

A New Age for the Farmer

There are three basic industries in the world: growing things, making things, and carrying things. Farming is the first important industry. At the present time farming needs to be completely revolutionized. The poor farmer—owning a few acres, a house, a barn, a few odd buildings, some horses, and a few cows, pigs, and chickens, and farming in the old way—cannot hope to rise very high in the economic scale. Even with the automobile and radio, life on the farm still has its drudgery, especially if there is a large family to bring up, take care of, and feed. Under present conditions there is no chance for a farmer to get ahead very fast, unless he uses new methods.

Large corporations, whose sole business it will be to perform the operations of plowing, planting, cultivating, and harvesting, will supersede the individual farmer, or groups of farmers will combine to perform their work in a wholesale manner. This is the proper way to do it and the only way in which economic freedom can be won.

[1] From Henry Ford, *My Philosophy of Industry*, authorized interviews by Fay Leone Faurote (New York: Coward-McCann, Inc., 1929), pp. 8–13, 56–61, 95–98, 101–7.

Power and machinery on the farm will make big production possible and solve the so-called "farmers' problem." Under these new conditions the pleasure of living in the country will return, and with faster and faster methods of transportation, the improvement of the radio, and the coming of television, the lonesomeness of farm life will disappear and only the pleasurable qualities remain.

Furthermore, man power will be released to carry on the two other great industries—manufacture and transportation—and by this means their cost will ultimately be reduced, waste eliminated, prices lowered, with the result that the general welfare of the world will be still further extended.

Repairing Men Like Boilers

Food is one of the most important commodities with which we have to deal. I am becoming more convinced every day that we should spend more time in the study of food and how to eat it. Most of us eat too much. We eat the wrong kind of food at the wrong time and ultimately suffer for it. We must find a better way to feed ourselves and provide our bodies with what they need for replenishment and growth. Hitherto we have spent more time in studying methods of repairing machinery and of renewing mechanisms than we have in studying this fundamental problem of human life. Of course, much has been done by our dietetists, but they have only scratched the surface. One does not have to be a food faddist to be interested in the subject.

Although the normal average life of human beings has been almost doubled in the last fifty years, I feel sure that we shall find means of renewing the human body so that men will retain their health, vitality, and mental keenness for many years longer. Take Edison, for example; today he is just as keen mentally as he ever was. There is every reason to believe that we should be able to renew our human bodies in the same manner as we renew a defect in a boiler. Not so long ago we found that our boilers were being discarded because in one or two spots corrosion had set in and weakened the surface.

We had some research work done on the problem and soon found a way to renew this metal at the point of expected failure, so that it was just as good as new. The boiler was put back into operation stronger, if anything, than when it was first installed. We have found ways to cut down corrosion and to limit deterioration by electrolysis, ways to prevent rust. The new chromium-plating process which we are using on airplane parts, for example, makes this metal practically indestructible in so far as the influence of weathered conditions on it is concerned. Rust-proof metals are being developed, we are finding ways to preserve wood, means of strengthening and preserving steel.

The point is, if there is enough thinking done along this line, there is no reason why we could not do the same with the human body. There is no law against it. The great problem is to get people in the mental attitude where they are willing to try to do it, willing to use the facts after we get them. There is a certain amount of mental inertia to be overcome in the promotion of any new thing. A few individuals may be quickly educated, but it takes time for society to move, to consent to the adoption of the new way.

*   *   *

Success

Students of world progress recognize that there is a time for everything. Like the opening of a flower or the budding of a tree, certain events cannot be forced ahead of their time; nor, conversely, can they be disregarded after the time for their appearance has come. Therefore it behooves the man—especially the young man—who wishes to have his part in the progress of this world, to watch the signs of the times and be ready at the proper moment to take his place in the procession of human events.

Not only in industry, but in all lines of work is this so. In the scheme of progress each unit has its logical place, which no other can fill. As a case in point, the automobile and the airplane could not be successfully developed until the internal combustion engine had been invented. Earlier engines, such as steam engines, were too heavy; they weighed too much per horsepower to be practical for use in these two new vehicles of transportation. But with the coming of the internal combustion engine it was possible to concentrate in a small place and a small weight an enormous amount of power. Thus it enabled us to develop the automobile, and, later on, the airplane. One invention makes way for another; one discovery lights up the path ahead so that he who runs may read—and lead.

Similarly, the development of industry was long delayed because one link in the chain of progress was missing. When that had been forged, industry shot ahead to its present high rate of production. I refer to the matter of long-distance power transmission. Back in the days when machinery had to be run by steam or water power, cables and belts were the only means of power transmission. This meant that factories had to be located in the immediate neighborhood of the plant, or on the bank of the stream from which power was derived. The natural tendency was for industry to group itself around large sources of power. Thus centralization was brought about, and on its heels followed quantity production. The mere idea of quantity production was a great step forward, but its concentration was hampered by the very condition that had given rise to it. So long as centralization was necessary, so long as manufacturing could be carried on only by the limited number of factories that could crowd around the various sources of power, quantity production on the present scale was impossible.

The Missing Link in the Chain of Progress

Then within our knowledge—within our century—electricity was discovered. Electricity possessed this great advantage over all other kinds of power previously produced: it could be instantaneously transmitted over great distances by wire. Power could be generated in one spot and sent out to any number of factories all over the country. The necessity for centralization had been eliminated, and manufacturing went ahead on a larger scale than ever.

Light, heat, and power—think what has been accomplished by this one idea put into action! And the power age has barely begun. In our own shops we are constantly improving our method of manufacture, with an eye to efficiency, economy, and the safety and comfort of our employees. Belt transmission has been entirely supplanted by electrically driven machines, which frees us from the danger and annoyance of wheels and belts whirling overhead. Our furnaces, most of which are electrically heated, are so constructed and insulated that the men work in front of them without discomfort. There is no smoke or gas except in a few processes, and, in these, electric ventilators carry off all disagreeable odors and unhealthful fumes.

The increase in the scale of production does not mean that craftsmanship has gone. From the earliest times machines of some sort have been in use. It took craftsmen to make and use machines then, and it takes craftsmen now. The hand and the brain and the eye have functioned together ever since man came upon the earth. The hand-made age is still with us, but it has been refined and advanced until it stands on a higher plane than when men used wooden plows and primitive potters' wheels. We value the things of the past because of their association; they were steps toward those of the present. But as needs have grown, means of production have been increased and improved.

It has been asserted that machine production kills the creative ability of the craftsman. This is not true. The machine demands that man be its master; it compels mastery more than the old methods did. The number of skilled craftsmen in proportion to the working population has greatly increased under the conditions brought about by the machine. They get better wages and more leisure in which to exercise their creative faculties.

*   *   *

The Extravagance of Government Financing

Suppose we in the United States find ourselves with some public improvement work to do, the development of some of our natural resources. The usual way the government sets about doing this sort of thing is to issue bonds—say for thirty years—and to sell them to the highest bidder. Then they go ahead and hire workmen to do the job, pay them with the money received from the proceeds of the sale of bonds, and then at the end of thirty years pay back the bondholders together with interest. What happens in the process? In the first place, what makes the bonds valuable? Why are people willing to buy them? Well, because the United States Government stands behind them; in other words, the government is putting up security for its own loans, and the security which it puts up is nothing more nor less than the energy of wealth in its most productive form, i.e., natural resources. It is the best security in the world, security that survives the wreck of banks and treasuries.

So then, if we start with a security which is unquestioned and which the people are willing to accept as collateral for the bonds issued, why should we go through the complicated and unnecessary process of paying 120 per cent interest out of our own pocket to somebody else for the privilege of getting $30,000,000 which, in reality, we already own? Take a piece of paper and a pencil and figure it out for yourself. Suppose we borrow $30,000,000 and pay 120 per cent interest, we literally have to pay $66,000,000 for the use of the $30,000,000. That is, we pay $30,000,000 for the public improvement and $36,000,000 for the loan. And it was the government's own money to begin with! It seems like a very childish and unbusinesslike method.

Now here is a way I see by which our government can get great work completed on a less complicated plan. It is a sound way, but there is one thing hard about it; it is so simple and easy that maybe some people can't see it. Suppose, for example, we desire to relieve unemployment by carrying on some necessary public improvement, and to do this the government needs $30,000,000. That's a million and a half twenty dollar bills or three million ten dollar bills. The government can issue these against the value of the thing in prospect and with them pay every expense connected with the work, then put the plant in operation and out of its earnings retire the entire $30,000,000 worth of currency which has been issued. Economists no longer question that method of doing things.

Indeed, it looks as if financial engineering will come round to something very like it. We shall see great improvement when we apply engineering methods to finance.

* * *

Business Men as Social Leaders

Business men do not think of themselves as leaders in social movements, but they are. Not a single system of business exists—good or bad—but has been taught to the people by business men. They have more influence on society than politicians, schoolmasters, or clergymen, because their contact is constant and their influence unavoidable. Every bad habit of unthrift and debt is taught the people by their business guides. Their leadership should turn around and head in the opposite direction. Business men should be readers of the signs of the times to warn the people to wise action and safe building on sound foundations. To be a business man is to assume the responsibility of economic leadership. No wrong economic practice, no disastrous system of doing business could possibly get a foothold except through the local business man.

There is no dangerous business practice in existence today that was not deliberately taught to the people, forced upon the people, by men who had no thought of the general social benefit. Teaching and leading the people to invest wisely, to begin getting things that make their lives more productive of real values is one thing; teaching them to forget their natural abhorrence of debt, leading them to forego their independence by working for a small army of installment collectors is quite another thing. If the careful, constructive attitude of the average family toward its economic responsibilities has been lowered, it is the result of systematic false education by a certain type of business system.

Now, when these things begin to appear and to flourish, the wise man sees a sign of coming danger and prepares for it. Systems wrongly based cannot succeed; they must fail and the colossal extent of everything we do in America brings the failure earlier and makes it harder than it would otherwise be. The self-limited business can weather any gale, but vast enterprises built on a gamble of other people's extravagance collapse at once. People who can see the signs of the times begin their own reformation. Those who are in places of leadership lend their good counsel. If the signs are observed soon enough, the situation is changed and we have gained some experience which will prevent a repetition of the mistake.

At present there is far less poverty in this country than ever before. Our material life is on a much higher level than it has ever been. But comparing the present with what it ought to be and what it could be, we cannot fail to see that much is yet to be done. Far more people, however, can be persuaded to relieve poverty than to devote their energies to removing it. Charity is no substitute for reform. Poverty is not cured by charity, it is only relieved. To cure it the cause of the trouble must be located and then removed. Nothing does more to abolish poverty than work. Every man who works is helping to drive poverty away.

It is not the men who are doing the talking who are solving our problems, but the men who are at work. Nobody can think straight who does not work, for idleness warps the mind. It is a wonder that we do not hear more about that fact, that the practiced hand gives balance to the brain. Thinking which does not connect with constructive action becomes a disease. The man who has it sees crooked; his views are lopsided. No man can think out our great problems for us. We believe in democracy because we believe that the collective mind is better than the single mind. With the people thinking together and planning together and acting together the greatest advances are possible.

Every age teems with theories requiring only to stand a while before their falsity will be revealed. We don't have to test every theory that is offered. Let it stand. If it is right, it will endure; if it is wrong, the public mind simply outgrows it. No one can imagine how much worse off we should be if we followed every theory and every leader that promised us the Golden Age. So if our progress seems slow, it is only because of the people's carefulness not to make a misstep. But there is progress being made at all times, now in this direction and now in that. Such progress is a social creation. It is the people moving up, and that is the only kind of progress there is. If we have not yet gone forward rapidly, there is a very great fact to be set against that fact: the human race has not had to retrace many steps because of false moves.

THE ECONOMIC SIGNIFICANCE OF THE AUTOMOBILE [2]

The present era of comparative prosperity coincides with the development of automotive transport. That has developed many millions of mobile horsepower and this in turn has caused a start toward rebuilding the country. It is responsible for the making over of thousands of miles of roads and for the building of thousands of new sections adjacent to cities. It has spread out the cities, but also it has brought the farm closer to the town. The single matter of giving people a chance to move about and see the world is an element which of itself would be sufficient to change the character of the people.

The results of this development—at the best only a partial development

[2] From *Moving Forward*, pp. 113–14, 243–45. Reprinted by permission of Mrs. Mary Owens Crowther.

—give an idea of what may come about with a fuller development. Or, instead of "fuller development," one might say the opening of wider opportunities.

It is not logical to divide the country into agricultural and industrial groups. Industry has already passed west to Chicago and beyond, while the South, which used to know only cotton, is now quickly becoming industrial because it is beginning to use its water resources for the generation of power. The shift is everywhere from wholly manufacturing or wholly agricultural to a balance between the two. If anyone would figure up the production of the small truck gardens, which so many factory workers may now have because of the automobile, the total would undoubtedly be astounding.

* * *

We believe that the automobile is in itself, both directly and indirectly, an important wealth-producing instrument, provided that it can be made so cheaply and so well that it can be put into the hands of the great mass of the population. It took the United States a long time to learn that the low-priced automobile was not simply a luxury that people would be better off without. We have seen the buying of automobiles pass down gradually from the higher ranges of wealth to a point where, by reason of a secondhand car at fifty or twenty-five dollars, anyone can own one. And we have seen the effects of this ownership on the prosperity of the country. The people of the United States do not own automobiles because they are prosperous. They are prosperous because they own automobiles and use them as tools to increase the range of their abilities.

That is one phase of the automobile, and it is peculiar to the automobile, but also there is the manner of its making that need not be peculiar to the automobile. It will apply to any commodity, and this method has by common consent been taken as fundamental to America's prosperity. The genesis of the method and its development have been explained at length in *My Life and Work* and in *Today and Tomorrow*; its further development has been explained in certain of its phases in the earlier chapters of this book. All that we have done or are today doing is open to the world to see. We have no secret processes and no magic formulas, but while the principles and their application are gradually becoming understood and followed in the United States they do not seem in every instance to be comprehended by the peoples from overseas.

We have been visited by many hundreds of foreign delegations, practically all of them searching for the secret of quick wealth. Not finding it they go away wondering. They seem not to comprehend the economy of the high wage or its influence upon consumption. Whether they be employers or whether they be workmen, the same thing is true. They do not comprehend; they simply say that we can do this or that because of the wealth inherent in the home market of the United States. They do not see that this is a *created* wealth, not merely a collected or accumulated wealth, and that our own company not many years ago was as small as a company could be, and that we have risen largely on the wealth that has been created through our service. Of course a company such as our own could not be built all at once simply by spending money. Ours is a development and not a promotion. The time element in our experience could not be duplicated for ten times our capital. No one can start where we are now, but the underlying principles of our policies have nothing to do with size. It is to demonstrate that prosperity can deliberately be produced that we have planted our roots in foreign soils—not primarily for our own benefit but because we believe we have an industrial method of bringing more comfort and more opportunity to people in the old lands.

5
War and History

Probably the best known of all the dicta attributed to Henry Ford is "History is bunk." He is supposed to have said it while he was testifying in his libel suit against the Chicago Tribune. *What he really said was quoted inaccurately and out of context. The origin of the statement was a remark by Ford in an interview with a* Tribune *reporter in 1916, in which the reporter, Charles N. Wheeler, was questioning Ford about his pacifist view. This interview was brought up during the libel suit and Ford was then questioned about it by his old antagonist of the Dodge case, Elliott Stevenson, who was now counsel for the* Tribune. *Stevenson also brought into his questioning a statement about history in an article by Theodore Delavigne, a Detroit journalist who in 1915 and 1916 prepared Ford's public statements on military and foreign policy. From the historian's point of view it is rather regrettable that Ford's counsel succeeded in shutting Stevenson off before Ford could testify about what histories he had read.*

"HISTORY IS MORE OR LESS BUNK" [1]

WHEELER: Henry Ford gave his views on disarmament straight from the shoulder. "But you're wrong there Mr. Ford," I argued. "Take England, for instance. For a thousand years they have been unable to invade this little strip of land you might tuck away in Michigan. Because England has a navy. Napoleon, with all of Europe at his feet, couldn't get across the twenty-one miles from Calais to Dover. What you ought to stand for is an American Navy. With an adequate Navy we could live in peace and security for a million years."

FORD: [According to Wheeler, Henry Ford had "a twinkle in his eye" at this point—ed.]
Say, what do I care about Napoleon. What do we care what they did 500 or 1000 years ago? I don't know whether Napoleon did or did not try to get across there (to England) and I don't care. It means nothing to me. History is more or less bunk. It's tradition. We don't want tradition. We want to live in the present and the only history that is worth a tinker's dam is the history we make today.
That's the trouble with the world. We're living in books and history and

[1] Excerpts from an interview by Charles N. Wheeler, *Chicago Tribune*, May 25, 1916.

53

tradition. We want to get away from that and take care of today. We've done too much looking back. What we want to do, and do it quick, is to make just history right now.

The men who are responsible for the present war in Europe knew all about history. Yet they brought on the worst war in the world's history.

FORD TESTIMONY, JULY 15, 1919 [2]

Q. But outside of the Wheeler communication (*Tribune* interview) do you recall that you were announcing to the world that you did not believe in history, that it was only tradition, and you didn't care anything about it. That is true, isn't it?

A. Never served me very much purpose.

* * *

[Referring to statement in Delavigne article "In all the history of civilization I cannot find one man who has justified war."—ed.]

Q. Did you mean to support your argument by a reference to history, the thing that you said was bunk?

(objected to as incompetent)

A. I say Mr. Delavigne added that. I don't remember ever reading it.
Q. Those are not your sentiments?
A. Well, I don't know about that.
Q. What?
A. As regarding history?
Q. Yes.
A. I said I did not go much on history.
Q. You don't believe in history?
A. I don't say don't believe in it.
Q. Have you ever read history?
A. Myself? Quite a lot, yes.

(objected to as incompetent and immaterial)

Q. You say you have read history?
A. Quite a lot, yes.
Q. Do you recall what histories you have read?

(objected to: sustained)

"A UNITED STATES OF THE WORLD" [3]

Machinery, The New Messiah

Machinery is accomplishing in the world what man has failed to do by preaching, propaganda, or the written word. The airplane and radio

---

[2] From State of Michigan, Circuit Court for the County of Macomb. Transcript of Testimony, Henry Ford v. Chicago Tribune Co., VIII, 5277, 5726.
[3] From *My Philosophy of Industry*, pp. 18–19, 46–47.

know no boundary. They pass over the dotted lines on the map without heed or hindrance. They are binding the world together in a way no other systems can. The motion picture with its universal language, the airplane with its speed, and the radio with its coming international programme—these will soon bring the whole world to a complete understanding. Thus may we vision a United States of the World. Ultimately, it will surely come!

*   *   *

Our new forms of transportation are making it easy for people to get out to see other localities, to become familiar with the kind of country in which they wish to settle. Such an interchange of social contacts, such a broadening of all people's geographical horizons will ultimately bring about a redistribution in which each person will naturally gravitate to that part of the country in which he is best satisfied to live. The automobile has done for this country what the airplane and radio may do for the world. A wider circulation of right ideas always breaks down prejudices and helps secure universal understanding.

This, then, suggests a solution of the problem of world peace. A peaceful nation is one that has the means to make war and refrains. Until the means are present, disposition toward their misuse cannot be fully known. In the present world the believers in peace confront the advocates of war and, fortunately, the former are better armed. Their power for peace seems to be in proportion to their power to enforce it.

6

Anti-Semitism [1]

One of the saddest episodes of Henry Ford's life was the anti-Jewish campaign that he began in his newspaper, the Dearborn Independent, *in 1920. No one has ever satisfactorily explained why he committed this folly. It is painfully evident from the defense given here that Ford himself had no understanding of what he was doing.*

The work which we describe as Studies in the Jewish Question, and which is variously described by antagonists as "the Jewish campaign," "the attack on the Jews," "the anti-Semitic pogrom," and so forth, needs no explanation to those who have followed it. Its motives and purposes must be judged by the work itself. It is offered as a contribution to a question which deeply affects the country, a question which is racial at its source, and which concerns influences and ideals rather than persons. Our statements must be judged by candid readers who are intelligent enough to lay our words alongside life as they are able to observe it. If our word and their observation agree, the case is made. It is perfectly silly to begin to damn us before it has been shown that our statements are baseless or reckless. The first item to be considered is the truth of what we have set forth. And that is precisely the item which our critics choose to evade.

Readers of our articles will see at once that we are not actuated by any kind of prejudice, except it may be a prejudice in favour of the principles which have made our civilization. There had been observed in this country certain streams of influence which were causing a marked deterioration in our literature, amusements, and social conduct; business was departing from its old-time substantial soundness; a general letting down of standards was felt everywhere. It was not the robust coarseness of the white man, the rude indelicacy, say, of Shakespeare's characters, but a nasty Orientalism which has insidiously affected every channel of expression—and to such an extent that it was time to challenge it. The fact

[1] From *My Life and Work*, pp. 250–52. Reprinted by permission of Mrs. Mary Owens Crowther.

that these influences are all traceable to one racial source is a fact to be reckoned with, not by us only, but by the intelligent people of the race in question. It is entirely creditable to them that steps have been taken by them to remove their protection from the more flagrant violators of American hospitality, but there is still room to discard outworn ideas of racial superiority maintained by economic or intellectually subversive warfare upon Christian society.

Our work does not pretend to say the last word on the Jew in America. It says only the word which describes his obvious present impress on the country. When that impress is changed, the report of it can be changed. For the present, then, the question is wholly in the Jews' hands. If they are as wise as they claim to be, they will labour to make Jews American, instead of labouring to make America Jewish. The genius of the United States of America is Christian in the broadest sense, and its destiny is to remain Christian. This carries no sectarian meaning with it, but relates to a basic principle which differs from other principles in that it provides for liberty with morality, and pledges society to a code of relations based on fundamental Christian conceptions of human rights and duties.

As for prejudice or hatred against persons, that is neither American nor Christian. Our opposition is only to ideas, false ideas, which are sapping the moral stamina of the people. These ideas proceed from easily identified sources, they are promulgated by easily discoverable methods; and they are controlled by mere exposure. We have simply used the method of exposure. When people learn to identify the source and nature of the influence swirling around them, it is sufficient. Let the American people once understand that it is not natural degeneracy, but calculated subversion that afflicts us, and they are safe. The explanation is the cure.

This work was taken up without personal motives. When it reached a stage where we believed the American people could grasp the key, we let it rest for the time. Our enemies say that we began it for revenge and that we laid it down in fear. Time will show that our critics are merely dealing in evasion because they dare not tackle the main question. Time will also show that we are better friends to the Jews' best interests than are those who praise them to their faces and criticize them behind their backs.

7
Prohibition and Morality[1]

Since Henry Ford disapproved of the use of both alcoholic beverages and tobacco, he naturally supported the Eighteenth Amendment. The opinions cited here were expressed in 1929. They show an unrealistic appraisal of the situation at that time, but Ford was no more misled about the future of Prohibition than many others. His views on this topic, and on morality in general, show his propensity to make industrial efficiency his ultimate standard of judgment.

Benefits of Prohibition

The gap between the people and their leaders is nowhere more discernible than in the matter of liquor. Some leaders are still for it; the people are now, as they have ever been, against it. The United States is dry not only legally but by moral conviction. You must find the people's sentiment where the people live. The American home is dry, and the American nation gets its tone from the home and not from the wet propagandist. In common decency the liquor generation should be allowed to die in silence. Its agonies should not be the constant topic of American journals.

Prohibition was intended to save the country and generations yet to come. There are a million boys growing up in the United States who have never seen a saloon, and who will never know the handicap of liquor, either in themselves or their relatives; and this excellent condition will go on spreading itself over the country when the wet press and the paid propaganda of booze are forgotten. There should be no mistake about it. The abolition of the commercialized liquor trade in this country is as final as the abolition of slavery. These are the two great reforms to which moral America committed itself from the beginning of its history.

Anything that interferes with our ability to think clearly, lead healthy, normal lives, and do our work well will ultimately be discarded, either as an economic handicap or from a desire for better personal health.

[1] From *My Philosophy of Industry*, pp. 14–17, 30–35, 36–40.

Tobacco is a narcotic which is exacting a heavy toll from our present generation. No one smokes in the Ford industries. Tobacco is not a good thing for industy nor for the individual.

The coming of prohibition has put more of the workman's money into savings banks and into his wife's pocketbook. He has more leisure to spend with his family. The family life is healthier. Workmen go out of doors, go on picnics, have time to see their children and play with them. They have time to see more, do more—and, incidentally, they buy more. This stimulates business and increases prosperity, and in the general economic circle the money passes through industry again and back into the workman's pocket. It is a truism that what benefits one is bound to benefit all, and labor is coming to see the truth of this more every day.

* * *

Our experiences are coming faster than ever before, both in our industrial world and in our domestic life. Many people see in these changes a world constantly growing worse. I do not believe this; I think we are headed in the right direction and that we should learn to interpret our new life rather than protest against it. We are entering a new era. Old landmarks have disappeared. Our new thinking and new doing are bringing us a new world, a new heaven, and a new earth, for which prophets have been looking from time immemorial. Much of it is here already. But I wonder if we see it.

I have no sympathy with those people who believe the world is growing worse. Of course, we all are making mistakes, but we learn by them. It is only when we correct these mistakes, reverse our tracks, and get back on the main road that we make progress. Automobiles that were made fifteen years ago no longer satisfy. We have all progressed, our needs have changed. We demand more, we see a wider horizon, a better type of civilization; and whether you believe that we are the originators of it or whether a wiser destiny has forced us to accept that which best promotes our welfare matters not. That fact is here and we must recognize it and conform our manner of living to it.

The basic things are, of course, very old. Nothing useful ever passes away. If a lightheaded group comes along and imagines they have found a new morality and if they draw to their books and plays and strange philosophies a following of other lightheaded groups, some serious people are inclined to believe that that old morality has passed away. The good old type of goodness they say is gone. It is a rather foolish position to take and causes needless worry.

There is nothing new except a new appreciation, a new understanding, and this is the result of experience, and the result of experience can only be character. I believe that all we are here for is to get experience and form our character. Although our beginnings may be small, yet daily we are adding to our sum total of knowledge of reality—those eternalities of which real life is composed. I believe that our conscious individuality will never be lost. No matter what plane of thought we may inhabit we shall be in full consciousness of our birthright of thinking, and by each experience we shall improve our character.

Unfortunately, there exists in our day the pretense of a curious prejudice against any view of life that presupposes moral laws or values. The word "moral," like many other terms, has been narrowed in its meaning so that it has been made to serve in the very opposite sense. But when one regards the moral law as merely the law of right action or of truth it becomes quite different from "trying to be good." The universe is set in a certain direction, and when you go along with it, that is "goodness." If you don't, you are getting an admonitory kind of experience.

There is a vast difference between a man's being merely statically "good" and being dynamically good. In one state he is merely good negatively, and in the other he is good for something and puts that goodness into effect. He accomplishes something for mankind. We make no progress so long as we deny this. Our motive cannot be the attainment of some kind of goodness which is apart from life itself, but the attainment of inherent rightness, physically, mentally, spiritually, so that this complex instrument which we call society may efficiently function. The right way is the only way. The rightness of an attitude or method goes down through all its relations. Rightness in mechanics, rightness in morals are basically the same thing and cannot rest apart.

*   *   *

Morality is merely doing the sound thing in the best way. It is a larger view and a longer view applied to life. The world is on the whole quite receptive to this implication of progress and we are all waiting for more manifestations of its workings, which are incidentally more numerous now than they have ever been in all the ages of mankind. Regardless of what we name it, this view is surely moving to practical recognition. There is one thing that we know about universal law: it operates for us if we will, against us if it must—but it operates.

Furthermore, I believe that the application of this law is necessary for business success. Just as a clean factory, clean tools, accurate gauges, and precise methods of manufacture produce a smooth-working, efficient machine, so clear thinking, clean living, square dealing make of an industrial or domestic life a successful one, smooth-running and helpful to every one concerned. It has always been surprising to me that so few people realize this great fact. Many people are led astray by gaudily painted substitutes, imitations, when they could have the genuine for the same equivalent of time or money—in fact, many times for much less.

The whole industrial world is suffering from many bad practices which we must refuse to use or tolerate. There must be a substitution of right methods, of right motives, the real ideas of service. I am no sentimentalist in this regard, it is just good business. There was a word once spoken which throws light on this: "Seek ye first the kingdom of God and His righteousness and all these things shall be added unto you." This is from the Sermon on the Mount. It sounds religious but it is just a plain statement of facts. It means just what it says—the reign, the rule, the law of the highest relations. Get that right way, work by that, and you have the world—a world without poverty, without injustice, without need.

As people wake up in their thinking—and we are even now arriving at this point in some respects—the benefits will be universally ours. Such facts are spreading throughout the whole civilized world. Even foreign lands are feeling the benefit of American progress, our American right thinking. Both Russia's and China's problems are fundamentally industrial and will be solved by the application of these right methods of thinking, practically applied.

Another thing, it is a mistake to think that we are living in a *machine age*. That's one of those bugaboos which people who do not understand the changing fundamentals of our civilization have set up. They prophesy all sorts of things because we have been freeing men for centuries and making it possible for them to widen their lives. We are *not* living in a machine age, *we are living in the power age*. This power age of ours has great possibilities, depending upon how we use it. Of course it can be abused. But it can also be used greatly to benefit mankind.

Here is where what we call the moral law comes in. Power must be properly used or it will destroy us. But I, for one, do not believe that we are headed in this direction. I believe that, fundamentally, every man has sensed his freedom and is eagerly making way for the new era, which is fast appearing.

FORD VIEWED BY HIS CONTEMPORARIES

Henry Ford attracted attention. He liked publicity and sought it *consciously, but even if he had been an inarticulate recluse he would still have been a figure of world-wide interest. The glamor of "Tin Lizzie," the technological revolution of the moving assembly line, the five-dollar, eight-hour day were bound to make him a marked man. Above all, here was a farm boy with little in the way of formal education who had built an enormous industry, kept it under his own control, and became a billionaire. Later, when the magic seemed to be less effective, the rigors of Ford's labor policies and his bitter opposition to unionization made him, in the eyes of his critics, the personification of everything that was wrong with American business.*

Millions of words were written about Henry Ford during his lifetime, expressing opinions covering the whole spectrum from uncritical adulation to uncritical condemnation, by individuals who knew what they were talking about and a good many more who did not. Rather than make the futile attempt to sample the mass, it seems preferable to present Henry Ford as he was seen by a few knowledgeable and well-informed observers. These selections include appraisals of Ford at the peak of his prestige and in decline, along with analyses of his industrial accomplishments by both administrative and legislative agencies of the government.

8
Ford at Zenith

When Ford's production miracle burst on the world, the novelty of his methods naturally aroused intense curiosity among engineers and production men, who wanted to know just how the feat was achieved. The following excerpts are from a study made initially for The Engineering Magazine *and then published separately. Horace L. Arnold was an industrial engineer and Fay L. Faurote a writer.*

THE INTRODUCTION OF THE MOVING ASSEMBLY LINE [1]

Beyond all doubt or question, the Ford Motor Company's plant at Highland Park, Detroit, Michigan, U.S.A., at the time of this writing is the most interesting metalworking establishment in the world—because of its size (something over 15,000 names on the payroll); because it produces one single article only (the Ford motor car) for sale; because the Ford Motor Company is paying very large profits (something like $15,000,000 a year); and because, with no strike and no demand for pay increase from its day-wage earners, the Ford Company made a voluntary and wholly unexpected announcement January 5, 1914, that it would very greatly increase day-pay wage and would at the same time reduce the day-work hours from nine to eight.

The Ford Motor Company is under one-man control, Henry Ford, head of the company, holding 58-1/2 per cent of the $2,000,000 capital stock; and it was Mr. Ford's own initiatory proposal to augment day-pay largely while reducing work-day hours from nine to eight, with an entire disregard of the commercial features of the situation—simply and solely with a view to the increased happiness and self-respect of his workmen, and in the face of Ford Company dividend reductions made the "Ford bonus" announcement, as first published in the Detroit afternoon papers of Monday, January 5, 1914.

Employers of labor the world over burst into a torrid eruption of denunciatory comment over the Ford bonus as soon as it became generally known, giving no heed whatever to its stated cause—a desire to better the condition of day-pay earners by wage increase, and to augment the number of day-pay workers by shortening the work day from nine hours to eight hours, all as given out by the company at the time of first announcement. The Ford Motor Company turns out one thousand automobiles per day at its Highland Park plant; two other plants, one at Ford, Ontario, Canada, and one at Manchester, England, bring the total Ford car-producing capacity to at least 1,200 cars per day, and the company has a world-wide selling and service organization which ensures the sale of its cars up to production capacity limit.

* * *

[1] From H. L. Arnold and F. L. Faurote, *Ford Methods and the Ford Shops* (New York, The Engineering Magazine Company, 1915), pp. 1–3, 16–18, 31–33, 112, 135–36, 137–39.

Henry Ford's character is extremely simple, and extremely easy to read; he is perfectly frank, is wholly self-reliant, is extremely affectionate and confiding by nature, is absolutely sure he is right in every wish, impulse and fancy, places no value whatever on money, and has a passion for working in metals and particularly for devising and building mechanically driven wagons to run on the ground or on common roads. His sense of humor is keen and he is ready to touch with his hands the men whom he likes. He has no sense of personal importance, meets his factory heads on terms of absolute and even deferential comradeship, and because he had, up to about his thirty-fifth year, an intimate personal knowledge of day-wage life, his strong natural impulse to aid his workmen and bring some chance of happiness into their lives takes the form of increasing day-pay and shortening labor-hours of his own motion, without waiting to be stimulated by demand from others for such action on his part.

Mr. Ford is by nature a comrade; and this, together with his sense of humor, leads him to smile often and much and to enjoy a laugh at his own expense, and he is rather inclined to underrate his own abilities and his own achievements. Socially, he likes men, especially young men and boys, and has a deep affection for wild animals and birds and flowers growing, which leads him to dislike to see animals or birds in captivity, and to dislike to see flowers cut from their roots.

War, battle, killing, and bodily mutilation are all alike abhorrent to Henry Ford, who lives a life of absolute freedom himself, following his own desires, fancies, and impulses with utter and absolute disregard of the opinions of others, as do all artists and originators and men of achievement.

As to literature, Mr. Ford may be said to have no literary tastes or inclinations whatever. He cares nothing for fiction, nothing for poetry, nothing for history and very little for scientific works, but has a strong liking for epigram, for short sayings which say much and include sharp contrasts. He abhors letters, and will not read a two-page letter through if he can possibly avoid it.

Henry Ford was the first-born child of two ardent lovers of mature age, both children of the soil. He was a child of great and absolutely faithful and constant love, and is therefore what he is, a strict monogamist by nature, strongly interested in homeless young boys, of whom he cares for a considerable number at Dearborn. He follows his own self-imposed tasks without one thought of looking back, unconscious of obstacles in his chosen path and careless of reward at the end of his labors, so that he but follow his ideal and reach the goal he has set for himself.

In person Henry Ford is full medium height, spare, active, goes bareheaded, perfectly healthy; he is wholly self-reliant, a law and a gospel to himself, a man of incredible capacity for work with his own hands, and governed in his social life by a deep sympathy for all free living things and especially for young things.

Henry Ford's rightful Coat of Arms is a file and hammer crossed, with a glowing heart above and the motto "I love," "I build," and "I give," in the side and bottom space.

Being what he is here said to be, what his biographical sketch shows him to be, and what his birth inexorably determined he should be, Henry Ford is an inventor, a creator, a master mind with a vivid imagination whose dictates he follows relentlessly; a generous comrade, making strong friends and willing servants of those whom he takes into his confidence, quick to praise the young men who are his factory aids and who are constantly encouraged by him in their strongly individualized and highly successful efforts towards bringing the Highland Park plant to that condition of Ideal Efficiency which is the never-to-be-fully-attained ambition of the competent factory manager at large.

* * *

It is absolutely correct to say that the Ford Highland Park shops are unique. The place certainly stands alone in three vital particulars, which dominate the practice at every point:

First, the company has but one solitary item of commercial product, the Ford motor car, made in one form only, because the differing body forms do not in any way modify the single chassis.

Second, the entire human race desires to ride, and to ride fast and cheaply, and the Ford car meets these conditions of human desire more suitably than any other automobile meets them, and hence is truly and in every sense a certain money-maker.

Third, the Ford car holds so closely to the one unchanged model that it becomes commercially possible to equip the shops with every special tool, great or small, simple or complex, cheap or costly, which can be made to reduce production labor-costs.

* * *

These three points of generic distinction—first, that the factory produces but a single article for sale; second, that it is an article of universal human desire, sold for cash to within 10 per cent of the total volume of production the moment it is completed; third, that being exempt from commercial demand for change of form, this article can be built through special machine-tool equipment of enormous cost—these three extraordinary characteristics place the Ford shops in a class by themselves for their certainty of money-making and exemption from rivalry with their product or competition for their gains.

These are not merely unconsidered assertions made in the interests of the Ford Motor Company. On the contrary they are the carefully matured conclusions of a widely inclusive search for the ultimate causes of the profits which compel a steady flow of vast sums of money through the Ford treasury, day in and day out, the whole year round.

The motor car had its epoch of opportunity, and Henry Ford was fortunate enough to make the car best fitted of all cars of its date to seize this opportunity, and to give this car sufficient vitality and stamina to enable it to hold what it grasped. He who best supplies a universally existent human desire has Fortune at his feet, as all students of commercial success are well aware. Mankind at large will surely purchase whatever meets its desires, and the lower the price the wider the field of sale. That is the foundation of trade at large, and what is here said of the true cause of the Ford car success cannot possibly be controverted.

The Ford factory holding thus, as it certainly does, a position commercially unique, may be safely expected to show very marked features of factory practice, wholly unlike the practice of any other existing factory, because the practice of every factory must be dominated by commercial conditions solely, if it is to continue in active existence, and the Ford factory does not disappoint those who expect to find its practice unique at vital points.

The urgent demand for maximum production is the dominant condition which governs every activity of the Highland Park shops. It is true that the automobile trade at large has its dull trade season of the year, that the spring and summer sales of motor cars vastly exceed those of the fall and winter, so far as the purchases of actual car-users are concerned; but nothing of this season-of-the-year-governed call for cars is ever felt in the Ford shops to the extent of giving the factory a slack period. The Ford system of branches and local sales agents acts as a reservoir of production; so that, because the maximum yearly production of the Ford car-building shops has never yet equaled the prospective demand for cars in the near future, the Highland Park shops are always working to full capacity.

The Highland Park shops are very far from manufacturing the entire Ford car. A long list of components, both rough and finished, are purchased from outside suppliers, who produce and sell to the Ford Company the bodies, wheels, tires, coil-box units, carburetors, lamps, ninety per cent of the car-body painting, all drop forgings, all roller and ball bearings, grease cups, spark plugs, electrical conductors, gaskets, hose connections and clips, horn, fan belt, muffler pipe, and part of the bolts. It is the policy of the company to deal with several suppliers of the same component, to ensure supply by drawing from several sources (which certainty of supply could not be had from any single producer) and also to make possible avail of competitive advantages not to be had if the total orders were placed with a single producer only.

Because the Ford Motor Company has but one production unit, the Ford car, and because the commercial demand for these cars has been, from the very first up to now, in excess of the plant production supply, the Ford production order is largely a matter of form and anticipatory surmise, based, as to quantity, on the "best judgment" of the sales department.

This commercial condition of being always oversold must, of course, dominate the Ford factory activities in all directions, and does, in point of fact, make the fixing of a production limit by an inflexible production order an impossibility.

*　　*　　*

The first flywheel magneto moving assembling line was installed, ready for work, about May 1, 1913, but the desirability of general application of the moving assembly line to the Ford motor assembling and the chassis assembling was not at once fully conceded by all the Ford engineers.

This moving assembly line is of historical importance as being the first moving assembly placed in work anywhere, so far as revealed by information to date. It is, of course, possible, or perhaps probable is the better word, that the moving assembly line has been used somewhere in the world, but it is new to the Ford engineers and entirely novel to me. If the moving assembly line has been used elsewhere, probably this publication will bring the previous use to public knowledge.

The flywheel magneto-assembling story will not be told in full at this time. The Ford motor is the only one used for automobile driving which fires the charge by current generated by a magneto built directly on the flywheel, and hence sure to run as long as the flywheel revolves—which, of course, gives a more direct and certain magneto drive than can be had with a separate magneto, gear-driven from the motor crankshaft, after the usual practice. Besides this, the Ford flywheel magneto is a novel construction, and it is hoped that it may be fully described at a future date, but at this time such description is outside of the line of thought.

Previous to the installation of this moving magneto-assembling line, the Ford flywheel magneto had been a one-man assembly, each workman on this job doing all the assembling of one flywheel magneto and turning out from 35 to 40 completed assemblies per nine-hour day. The work was done by experienced men, but was not so uniformly satisfactory as was desired, and was costly as a matter of course, as all one-man assembling must of necessity be forever.

Forty assemblies per nine-hour day, best time for one-man work, gives nearly twenty minutes time to each one.

When the moving assembly line was placed in work with twenty-nine men, splitting the one-man operations into twenty-nine operations, the twenty-nine men began turning out 132 magneto assemblies per hour, or 1,188 per nine-hour day, one man's time producing one flywheel magneto assembly in thirteen minutes ten seconds, a saving of nearly seven minutes time on each assembly, or more than one-third of the best one-man time.

*   *   *

The Ford chassis assembling in moving lines affords a highly impressive spectacle to beholders of every class, technical or nontechnical. Long lines of slowly moving assemblies in progress, busy groups of successive operators, the rapid growth of the chassis as component after component is added from the overhead sources of supply, and, finally the instant start into self-moving power—these excite the liveliest interest and admiration in all who witness for the first time this operation of bringing together the varied elements of the new and seemingly vivified creation, on the three Ford chassis-assembling lines where over 1,200 have been put together and driven out of doors into John R Street in one single eight-hour day.

Up to August, 1913, the Ford chassis was assembled in one location. First the front and rear axles were laid on the floor, then the chassis frame with springs in place was assembled with the axles, next the wheels were placed on the axles, and the remaining components were successively added to complete the chassis. All components needed to make up one chassis had to be brought by hand to each chassis-assembling location. This routine of stationary chassis assembling was, in September, 1913, worked with two lines of assembling-floor space, 600 feet long, 12 feet chassis-to-chassis centers, 50 assembling locations in each 600-foot line, 100 cars in process of assembling in the two lines. Working in this routine 600 men were employed, 500 being assemblers who were supplied with components by 100 men acting as component carriers.

About April 1, 1913, the first sliding assembling line, used for assembling the Ford flywheel magneto, was placed in work and immediately showed a large reduction in assembling labor-cost. Consequently, the possibility of lowering chassis-assembling costs by introducing the moving assembling line for chassis assembling became a matter of discussion among the Ford engineers.

In the month of August, 1913 (the dull season) 250 assemblers, with a stationary assembling location for each chassis, the assemblers being served by eighty component carriers, worked nine hours per day for twenty-six days to turn out 6,182 chassis assemblies. Total labor hours $330 \times 9 \times 26 = 77,220$ hours, giving twelve hours and twenty-eight minutes for labor time on each chassis, about as good as was ever done with stationary chassis assembling.

The assembling line was long—600 feet—but even at that did not give room enough, and twelve and one-half hours of labor time seemed altogether too much for one chassis. It was in the dull season, and an experiment was made with rope and windlass traction on a moving assembly line 250 feet long. Six assemblers traveled with the chassis as it was slowly pulled along the floor by the rope and windlass past stationary means of component supply, and the chassis-assembling time was reduced to five hours and fifty minutes of one man's time, over fifty per cent saving.

October 7, 1913, on a moving assembly line 150 feet long, with no helpers, components being piled at suitable locations, 140 assemblers in the line completed 435 chassis assemblies in one nine-hour day, two hours and fifty-seven minutes of one man's time for each chassis assembling.

The assembling line was lengthened by degrees to 300 feet, giving the men more room, and on December 1, 1913, 177 assemblers working nine hours turned out 606 completed chassis assemblies, about two hours and thirty-eight minutes of one man's time to each chassis.

December 30, 1913, working two assembling lines, 191 men completed 642 chassis assemblies in one nine-hour day, a little less than two hours forty minutes of one man's time for each chassis, the cars being pushed along by hand.

January 14, 1914, one assembling line was endless chain-driven, with favorable results.

*   *   *

January 19, four chassis-assembling lines were worked, only one line being chain-driven. The wheels were put on as soon as the axles and the chassis frames were assembled, and the assemblies in progress ran with their front wheels on the floor and their hind wheels carried in three-wheeled cradles, used to give easy placing of the rear wheels on the motor-starting drive at the end of the line.

February 27, 1914, the first high line of rails with chain drive was used. The chassis slid on its axles as pulled by the chain, and the wheels were applied only a short distance before the motor-starting was reached. This first high line was made with rails 26-3/4 inches above the shop floor, and at once showed great advantages, the best time for one chassis assembling being only 84 minutes, while the worst time was two hours. Two other high lines were soon installed, 24-1/2 inches high, with chain drives; tall men worked on the line 26-3/4 inches high, and short men on the other two lines, 24-1/2 inches high.

The Ford engineers make a point of "man-high" work placing, having learned that any stooping position greatly reduces the workman's efficiency. The differing heights of the chassis-assembling high lines are believed to be decidedly advantageous.

On these three high lines, on April 30, 1914, 1,212 chassis assemblies were completed in one eight-hour day, each chassis being assembled in one hour thirty-three minutes of one man's time, as against twelve hours twenty-eight minutes, the best time with stationary chassis assembling, September, 1913—ninety-three minutes as against 728 minutes—and it must be borne in mind that the September, 1913 Ford practice in chassis assembling was fully abreast of the best known in the trade. Very naturally this unbelievable reduction in chassis-assembling labor costs gave pause to the Ford engineering staff, and led to serious search for other labor-reduction opportunities in the Ford shops, regardless of precedents and traditions of the trade at large.

The chassis was not completed when it ran out into John R Street, and the first practice was to let the driver run the chassis up and down until he thought best to abandon it to the motor inspector and the rear-axle inspector, and to return to the end of the assembling lines for another chassis to drive out into John R Street. The bodies were allowed to slide down an incline from the second floor, and were then dragged along the pavement by one man and stood on end in a bunch south of the chute.

When the assembly was completed on the John R pavement, and had been inspected by the motor inspector and the rear-axle inspector, it was again boarded by a driver and taken to the bunch of bodies, where four men lifted a body into place on the chassis, and the completed automobile assembly was then driven to the shipping clerk's office, between the railway tracks, ready for shipment.

"I HAVE KNOWN HENRY FORD FOR TWENTY YEARS" [2]

Few men were closer to Henry Ford during his period of zenith than the Reverend Dr. Samuel S. Marquis, dean of St. Paul's Cathedral (Episcopal) in Detroit. Ford himself had no religious beliefs; he took his ideas on this subject, as on others, mainly from his friend Edison. However, Mrs. Ford was an active member of Marquis' congregation, and her husband was a contributor. Dean Marquis was therefore a family friend. He tried to dissuade Ford from going on the "peace ship" expedition but went along with him when it was evident that Ford was determined to go.

In 1915, as he describes, Marquis replaced John R. Lee as head of the Sociological Department. This was an organization created for the purpose of

[2] From Samuel S. Marquis, *Henry Ford, An Interpretation* (Boston: Little, Brown and Co., 1923), pp. 4–8, 8–9, 15–16, 20–22, 31–35, 41–45, 49–50, 70–71, 90–91, 130, 147–51, 153–55, 164–67.

helping Ford workers meet the standards required to qualify for the five-dollar-a-day wage scale. It has usually been criticized as an agency whose basic function was to pry into the private affairs of Ford employees and compel them to comply with Henry Ford's rigid code of conduct. This criticism is less than fair. As long as Ford was interested in promoting the welfare of his workers and was willing to give Lee and Marquis a reasonably free hand, the Sociological Department was able to assist the large numbers of people who converged on Detroit to work for Ford to adjust to their new way of life. In addition, at a time when union organization in the automobile industry was not only nonexistent but scarcely dreamed of, the Sociological Department provided some protection for Ford workers against arbitrary action by foremen and supervisors.

I have known Henry Ford for twenty years. For a time he was my parishioner, and then for a time I was his employee.

Given freedom to create a man will reveal himself in what he produces —the painter in his picture, the sculptor in his marble, the writer in his book, the musician in his composition, and the mechanic in his machine. The Ford car is Henry Ford done in steel, and other things. Not a thing of art and beauty, but of utility and strength—the super-strength, power and endurance in engine and chassis, but somewhat ephemeral in its upper works. With top torn, body dented, upholstery gone, fenders rattling, and curtains flapping in the wind, you admire the old thing and speak softly and affectionately of it, because under the little hood the engine— occasionally on four, sometimes on three, frequently on two, and now and then on one—keeps rhythmically chugging along, keeps going when by all the laws of internal combustible things it ought to stop and with one weary expiring gasp fall to pieces and mingle with the mire its few remaining grains of rust. But it keeps going, just as he keeps going contrary to all the laws of labor, commerce and high finance.

Some years ago I sat in the office of a Ford executive, discussing with him a certain thing the "chief" had ordered done. "It's a fool thing, an impossible thing," said the executive, "but he has accomplished so many impossible things that I have learned to defer judgment and wait the outcome. Take the Ford engine, for example; according to all the laws of mechanics the damned thing ought not to run, but it does."

As in the Ford engine, so in Henry Ford there are things that by all the laws of ordinary and industrial life should "queer" him, put him out of the running, but he keeps going.

He is an extraordinary man, a personality in the sense that he is different from other people, quite different, for that matter, from what he is popularly supposed to be.

But however unlike the rest of us Henry Ford may be in some respects, he falls under the classification of ordinary mortals in this: he is not satisfied with what he has and is.

He is one of the richest men on earth. He is the most widely known man in the industrial world. But with these things he is not content. He had other ambitions. For example, he not only has the willingness, but has shown a rather strong desire to assume national political responsibilities. And on one occasion he voluntarily took upon himself the task of settling the problems of a world at war. His ability to do in other than the industrial sphere may be commensurate with his will, but his efforts in other directions have not been such as to inspire confidence.

It is not only the absence of certain qualifications, but the presence of others that make us doubt his fitness for the field of politics. If our Government were an absolute monarchy, a one-man affair, Henry Ford would be the logical man for the throne. As President, and he seems to have aspirations in that direction, he would be able to give us a very economical administration, for a Cabinet and Congress would be entirely superfluous if he were in the White House. The chances are that he would run the Government, or try to do so, as he runs his industry, having had experience along no other lines. The Ford organization would be transferred to Washington. That would not be so difficult a matter as it might appear to the uninitiated. It could be accomplished in a single section of a Pullman car, with one in the upper and two in the lower berth. I agree with Mr. Edison, who was recently reported as saying of Mr. Ford, "He is a remarkable man in one sense, and in another he is not. I would not vote for him for President, but as a director of manufacturing or industrial enterprises I'd vote for him—twice."

But I doubt if the spark of political ambition in him ever would have burst into flame had it been left to itself. There are those near him, however, who never cease to blow upon it and fan it, being themselves ambitious to sit in the light of the political fire which by chance may be kindled in this way. They seem to entertain no doubt of their ability to run any office for him from that of the Presidency down.

But Henry Ford has left upon me the impression that his chief ambition is to be known as a thinker of an original kind. He has the not uncommon conviction among mortals that he has a real message for the world, a real service to render mankind.

*   *   *

In my opinion he could realize his supreme ambition if he were to follow the example of a good shoemaker and stick to his last, that is, to the human and production problems in industry and leave national, international and racial problems alone. It is human to grow weary of achievement in one direction. Like Alexander, we tearfully long for adventures in other worlds instead of trying to bring a little nearer to perfection the world we have conquered.

For many years Mr. Ford shunned the public gaze, refused to see reporters, modestly begged to be kept out of print; and then suddenly faced about, hired a publicity agent, jumped into the front page of every newspaper in the country, bought and paid for space in which he advertised what were supposed to be his own ideas (although he admitted in the *Chicago Tribune* trial that he had not even read much that had been put out under his own name) and later bought a weekly publication and began to run "his own page." I think he would rather be the maker of public opinion than the manufacturer of a million automobiles a year, which only goes to show that in spite of the fact that he sticks out his tongue at history, he would nevertheless not object to making a little of it himself.

This laudable ambition to serve the world, and, in some degree, to mold its thought, has very naturally aroused in men the desire to know more intimately this man who volunteers to take the part of Moses—he doesn't put it just this way—in a world-exodus into a new era of peace and prosperity. Having made himself a world figure, or persisting in being reckoned as one, the world insists, and properly so, on knowing all there is to know about him. It is the price every man must pay for aspiring to such an exalted position.

*   *   *

The ordinary mortal is content to hitch his wagon to a star. This is a sport too tame for Henry Ford. He prefers to hang on to the tail of a comet. It is less conventional, more spectacular and furnishes more thrills.

Mr. Ford seems to love sensations, to live in them and to be everlastingly creating them, jumping from one to another. And many of his sensational acts and utterances are so clever that the world looks on with something more than amusement. In spite of the fact that he has come near making a clown of himself on more than one occasion, the audience, for the most part, continues to watch him with wonder and admiration. He has been right so many times in industrial matters, done so many admirable and worthwhile things, that we are inclined to forget the times he has been wrong or foolish.

I suppose that an acrobat with a net under him takes risks that he would not take if he were looking down on the bare hard earth. In like manner, I suppose, the fact that one has under him several hundred millions to fall back on renders him more or less indifferent to a tumble. He can afford to try stunts he would otherwise hesitate to undertake. But whatever the reason, Henry Ford appears to be drawn to the limelight as a moth to a candle. If he comes out slightly singed, as in the case of the peace ship and the *Tribune* trial, he nevertheless comes gayly and boldly back to flutter around a Semitic or other candle. One cannot but marvel at the continuance of the public's patience, interest and faith.

*   *   *

But to the credit of Henry Ford it must be said that he has done sensational things of a higher and saner order. He had done a number of things in industry because he thought them right and just, and the world has labeled them sensational. But it was not the thing in itself that was sensational, but the fact that he had the courage to do it. It ought not to be counted a sensational thing that a man loves his wife, but in a community where it is supposed no man cares for his wife, it might create more or less of a sensation to find one who does. And surely such a man should not be charged with bidding for notoriety. Henry Ford has done many things in the handling of labor which, if all employers were doing by labor as they should, would not be counted sensational at all.

In 1914 Mr. Ford agreed with Mr. James S. Couzens, business manager of the Ford Motor Company until 1915 and later United States Senator from Michigan, that, in view of the earnings of the company, the men in their employ should be given an increase in pay. Mr. Couzens dared him to make the minimum pay five dollars a day, and Mr. Ford agreed. It was nothing more than a company in the financial position the Ford company was then in should do. Few, however, do it. Hence the sensation when Henry Ford did it.

He increases wages and at the same time reduces the cost of the car. Sensational! But why should it be considered a sensational thing to give the customer some of the benefits which the increasing prosperity of a company makes it possible to bestow? Why—except that few do it? Shrewd business? Good advertising? Certainly, it is all that, and more. There can be no greater shrewdness in business than to follow the laws of honest and just dealing, provided you expect to remain any length of time in business.

I went to the Ford Motor Company with the conviction that it pays in industry in the long run to do the thing that is right, just and humane. I left the company with that conviction more firmly fixed in my mind than ever. This universe is one, and the laws in one sphere of life are not in conflict with those of another. What is wrong out of business cannot be right within it.

*   *   *

I do not know how much Henry Ford is worth. I am under the impression that, if he so desired, he could convert his business into a stock company and pay very satisfactory dividends on a billion capitalization.

I doubt whether any other man ever made so large a fortune in so short a time. I believe it to be one of the cleanest, if not the cleanest, fortune of its size ever made.

As a rule, great wealth is quickly made by a gamble of some sort, or by investments in a highly favored and protected field, or by acquiring a monopoly of some natural resource, or by business methods which crush competition.

Henry Ford has made his money in a free, open, unprotected and competitive field.

The one possible blot on his record in this connection is the charge that he has sometimes dealt ruthlessly with smaller independent concerns which were making some parts of his car for him; that while he was paying his own labor a minimum wage of five and six dollars a day, he was demanding of others that they sell him their product at a price that made it impossible for them to pay their labor a fair wage; that he has encouraged men to make large investments in order to furnish him with materials, and then has suddenly ceased to place orders with them and left them with an idle investment and a deserted factory on their hands.

Perhaps his answer to this charge, if there is any truth in it, would be that even so, they made good money while they were going, and that he left them better off than when he found them; and as for the low wages paid their men, that was not due to the price he set for their output but to poor management and production methods; for later he was able to make the thing they were making for him at a cost less than he was paying them, and at the same time to pay five and six dollars minimum wage for the labor that went into it.

I have listened to many discussions on this point and am well aware that there is a sharp division of opinion in regard to it. The view one takes of it will depend almost entirely on what he considers fair in business, and on that men are a long way from agreement.

Henry Ford does not gamble. I once saw him win five cents on a bet. I took it away from him and put it into a charity fund so I know that tainted nickel is not mixed up with the other twenty billion nickels, more or less, now in his possession.

I once ran him a foot race on which we and our friends risked a small stake. Henry won. And I may say right here for the benefit of others more than fifty years of age and forty-two inches in circumference that you are not in Mr. Ford's class unless you have kept in excellent physical condition.

And I may add also, by way of finishing this story, that Mr. Ford took the money from those who won on this race and gave it to an old gatekeeper at a railroad crossing.

But this is aside. What I started to say was that the Ford fortune, as fortunes go, is clean. And it has been handled in a way that has caused neither criticism nor hatred on the part of the working classes. If there are any who would like to see Mr. Ford lose out, they are not in the ranks of labor.

He has been generous toward his employees. On this point I think I can speak with some authority, as I was in a position to know for a period of several years. During the time I was with the company he gave to his employees, in addition to a generous wage, more than a hundred million dollars out of his profits, all of which he could have retained as his own, and which the average man would have put into his own pocket.

It is said that his profit-sharing plan was a crafty scheme for getting more work out of his men; that it actually returned more dollars to him than he gave out. It was unquestionably a shrewd and profitable stroke. To the credit of Mr. Ford be it said that he personally never maintained that his profit and bonus schemes were a means for distributing charity.

I have often discussed the Ford Profit-Sharing Plan before groups of employers of labor. Seldom, if ever, have I done so that some man has not risen to ask, "Didn't the plan pay? And didn't Mr. Ford believe that it would pay? Would he have instituted it, if he had not believed it would bring more dollars to him?" And the answer was, "Certainly the plan pays. That is just the point I am trying to make. And I would further like to make it clear that the plan is not copyrighted. Any employer is at liberty to try it. Both for the sake of the employer and the employees, we would like to see others try it out."

*   *   *

Henry Ford has built up a great industry; he has amassed a great fortune; he has paid labor a liberal wage; he has built a hospital; he has set in operation agencies which in their day have done a great deal of good. To human thought, to politics, to science, the arts, education, religion, his contribution—directly or indirectly—is yet to be made.

What he has done for others has been along lines that have as a rule brought a liberal return to himself. Seriously and to his credit I would say that his most valuable contribution to humanity thus far has been his discovery of some very profitable kinds of philanthropy. A good thing done for reward is good. Nobler and better things, however, are possible. I wish Henry Ford had more good to his credit that had cost him something. In actual service to humanity and in unselfish use of his wealth his old running mate, Couzens, has done so far more that will live.

Henry Ford plays a spectacular game. He pulls some wonderful stunts. He is a pinch hitter in finance and the idol of the bleachers. But there are better all-round men in the game. He is as temperamental as an artist and as erratic. He has been known to fan out. And he certainly muffed a couple of balls in the case of the peace ship and his Jewish diatribes. He is not a team man. He must play the game alone and for himself. He has advanced a good many men on the bases of the financial diamond, but I do not recall that he ever did so by a sacrifice hit.

Henry Ford has attained a remarkable prominence, but he has not attained that which makes prominence permanent, namely, eminence. Prominence may be gained by saying things and doing things; eminence is achieved by being. The essence of eminence is a man—in his mind and soul. Henry Ford is an unusual, a most remarkable man, but not a great man—not yet. There are in him neither that breadth nor depth of mind, nor that moral grandeur which are the distinguishing marks of the truly great. Some men are born great, some achieve greatness, but no man ever had greatness thrust upon him, Shakespeare to the contrary. He may be thrust into prominence, but not into eminence, for eminence is reached by climbing an inward spiritual ascent.

If Henry Ford could quit watching the popular winds, take down his political lightning rod, and devote himself to the solution of those human problems which press upon him for solution as an industrial leader, I think he could attain a great and enviable reputation. It is in that direction, I believe, that he will find the fulfillment of the wish which he expressed to me when he said, "I do not want the things which can be bought with money. I want to live a life—to live so that the world will be better for my having lived in it." He has had the vision. He has the ability and the opportunity.

It is unfortunate that he has not manifested the same sustained interest in the work undertaken in behalf of his employees that he has shown in some other matters. In some things he reveals an indomitable will, an unfailing interest. In other things the will weakens and the interest dies. He sometimes springs at things with startling suddenness. And then he drops them as suddenly as he took them up. It requires a stronger will to be than to do.

In 1914 he entered with great enthusiasm a new path in the field of social justice. The work he then instituted gave promise of a notable contribution to human progress along industrial lines. It quickened the conscience of the employers. It roused hope in the ranks of labor. It promised the restoration of that which modern industry has lost and which would prove the greatest boon any man could restore to it, namely, a personal relation between employer and employee. That phase of the work, with some other distinguishing features of it, are for the present in eclipse; only in eclipse, it is to be hoped.

As to Henry Ford's success in industry, it is no mere accident. You cannot say that it is a matter of luck that a man's boat is floated by the rising tide, if he has carefully calculated the time the tide comes in and has built his boat where it would be caught and carried out to sea. Mr. Ford anticipated the rising tide of the automobile industry. He must be given credit for that. Credit also is due him for the way in which he deliberately planned to take the fullest possible advantage of the tide when it came in. Standardization is his hobby. He would have all shoes made on one last, all hats made on one block, and all coats according to one pattern. It would not add to the beauty of life, but it would greatly reduce the cost of living.

When it came to automobiles Henry Ford decided to make them all alike and of a size that would fit, not the greatest number of people, but the largest number of pocketbooks. Keep your eye on the average pocketbook. That was his slogan. Only a few people can buy what they want. The vast majority buy what they can afford. No one was ever able to shake him in his decision to make one car, the best of its kind that can be made for the money, suited to the bank roll of the greatest number of people, standardized so as to admit of quantity production and therefore of manufacture at minimum cost.

Once he got going he discovered and put into practice some very profitable ways of being generous. His division of profits with his employees paid in dollars and cents. That fact made it none the less a boon to labor. His policy of sharing some of his profits with the consumer by cutting the price of the car also paid. It widened his market and won the confidence and good will of the public. He did what no other man has ever been able to do—touched the hearts of the people through their pocketbooks.

He never went to college, but he knows all the psychology there is to know in so far as it has to do with the dollar.

*   *   *

A cross section of the mind of Henry Ford would reveal some striking contrasts. There are in him mental altitudes which mark him as a genius, and there are others that are little above mental sea level. A complex mind of strength and weakness, of wisdom and foolishness, in which the shallows are the more pronounced because of the profound depths which lie between.

Mr. Ford has limitations which stand out the more conspicuously because of the far reaches of his mind in other directions. He has altogether a most unusual mind—in some respects the most remarkable mind I have ever known. Call it insight, intuition, vision or what you please, he has a supernormal perceptive faculty along certain lines in business affairs.

His mind does not move in logical grooves. It does not walk, it leaps. It is not a trained mind. It does not know how to think consecutively, and I doubt if it would do so if it could. It cannot endure the pace and bear the burden of logic, and it cannot listen long to the man who is reaching conclusions through rational processes. I have known him frequently to cut in and give a man a decision before he has had time to state his case, and sometimes the decision has had nothing whatever to do with the case. Under such circumstances there was no use trying to get the real problem before him. A later opportunity must be waited for.

He does not reason to conclusions. He jumps at them. A bad thing, unless the jump, as in his case, is as a rule more unerring than the slow reasoned crawl of other minds. He has told me that he learned early in life "to grab the first hunch." His first impulses, so he insists, are as a rule to be relied upon and acted upon. He maintains that if he stops to reason about them, to discuss them, to seek advice regarding them, he finds them trimmed, pared and filed down until they fit into the conventional ruts, and there is nothing left that is really worth doing.

*   *   *

Once you get to Mr. Ford, you will find him, of all men, most affable and democratic. He is apt to leave upon you the impression that he stands ready to do anything for you, give you anything, even to the half of his kingdom. He makes promises which he sometimes keeps, sometimes forgets, and sometimes fulfills in his own peculiar way. He hates to say "No." He has a way of leaving you with the idea that he is in entire sympathy with your proposition and of delegating the unpleasant task of turning you down to someone else.

To turn down a request made of us is embarrassing. To grant a favor is a pleasure. Henry Ford is a man of generous impulses. I think he would prefer on all occasions to do what he is asked to do. This, of course, is impossible. And so, when it is necessary to turn a man down, he seeks to relieve himself of the embarrassment of doing so by referring the man to someone else, at the same time indicating just how he would have the man and his request handled. He has sometimes given a man a note to an executive, which was in reality a code letter understood by the official receiving it. That note was always the same with slight variations in the spelling of one word. The fate of the individual joyfully and unsuspectingly bearing that note hung on the spelling of that word. If the note read "Please s-e-e this man," it meant he was to be favorably handled. If it read "Please s-e-a this man," it meant that he was to be let down as easy as possible—dropped overboard into a sea of uncertainty, so far as obtaining what he wanted was concerned, there to wait and flounder about until, utterly discouraged, he gave up hope of attaining his end. It always seemed to me that a blunt "No" would have been a much more considerate way of dealing with cases of this kind.

Genial, generous and democratic will be found the manner of Henry Ford, once you get to him, but the problem is to get to him.

* * *

To sum it all up. Henry Ford is not a churchman in the sense that he attends any church with regularity, enters into its worship, sacramental or other, is interested in the extension of its work, and contributes toward its support in a manner commensurate with his means. His father was a vestryman in the little Episcopal church in Dearborn. It was in this church that Mr. Ford was baptized and confirmed.

Like many another man, baptized and confirmed in early life, he has not maintained a close contact with organized religion in later years. I cannot conceive of him working contentedly and enthusiastically in any organization, religious or secular, in which he is not the dominating spirit and majority stockholder. If he were to accept the authority and responsibility for the reorganization of the church along lines of efficiency and finance, I have no idea what he would do. But I am sure that whatever he did would go down in ecclesiastical history. Much that is now at the bottom would come to the top, so far as the organization is concerned, and much now at the top would sink into oblivion. We would have the unique spectacle of ecclesiastical conventions meeting annua'ly to devise ways and means for using a surplus, instead of assembling, as at present, for the purpose of working out some plan for meeting the deficit in last year's missionary budget. The clergy might be taken care of by giving them a job six days in the week in the foundry; with the understanding that they preach gratis on the seventh.

I cannot imagine Henry Ford interested in creeds, much less subscribing to one. He is disposed to do his own thinking in matters of religion as in other matters. Theology interests him, but it is not the kind that is found in the seminaries.

He is not an orthodox believer according to the standards of any church that I happen to know.

His religious ideas, as he states them, are somewhat vague. But there is in him something bigger than his ideas, something of a practical nature that is far better than his nebulous theories.

* * *

Henry Ford has millions in reserve, owes no man a dollar—and is hopelessly in debt.

If the Ford indebtedness were such that it could be met by writing a check it would have been paid in full long ago. But it isn't that kind of an obligation. There are things connected with the formation of his executive scrap heap which leave the impression that Henry Ford is more or less unfamiliar with some of the finer ways of expressing his appreciation of the services rendered him.

It is unfortunate that he has left the impression that the dollar is his favorite standard of measure when he comes to estimate the value of human service. I do not mean to say that he has never paid in any other way. In many instances he has shown friendly and generous consideration beyond the payment of a wage or salary to men in his employ.

In other instances men have been rewarded in a way that has left him in their debt. He has paid them liberally, given bonuses, bestowed costly gifts. They started poor with him and ended rich. They began in humble positions and were advanced to places of honor and responsibility and paid princely salaries. If they have gone into the scrap heap later, why should they complain? What more could he or any other man do for them than he had done?

But there are things in human relations which some men prize above money. There are ways of throwing a man on the scrap heap which leave him with a high regard and a friendly feeling for the man who threw him there.

*　　*　　*

It was toward the close of the year 1915 that I gave up the deanship of St. Paul's Cathedral, Detroit, and took charge of the Sociological Department of the Ford Motor Company. I continued in the employ of the company for a period of a little more than five years.

The Sociological Department—later known as the Educational Department—had been organized early in the year 1914, at the time the Ford profit-sharing plan, with its five-dollars-a-day minimum pay went into effect. To Mr. John R. Lee, who organized the department and conducted its work for the first two years of its existence, credit is due, more than to any other one man, for devising those unique humane policies which attracted world-wide attention, and which gave a practical and helpful direction to the philanthropic impulses of Mr. Ford. There is in Mr. Lee a rare combination of qualities which were needed at the time in the development of the personnel work of the company.

Mr. Ford has a way of making great things possible, of opening the door of opportunity for others. And fortunately for him, he has been able in the past to gather about him men who have been able to seize upon these opportunities and to use them in a way that has reflected great credit upon him and upon themselves. If it had not been for Mr. Lee, I am inclined to think that the sociological work of the Ford Motor Company would have taken its course along lower and conventional lines. He is a man of ideas and ideals. He has a keen sense of justice and a sympathy with men in trouble that leads to an understanding of their problems. He has an unbounded faith in men, particularly in the "down and outs," without which no man can do constructive human work. Under his guidance the department put a soul into the company and gave intelligent direction to the generous thought and will of Mr. Ford and Mr. Couzens toward their employees. Mr. Lee must be credited with being one of the makers of the Ford Motor Company on its human side.

A few days after the profit-sharing plan went into effect I called upon Mr. Ford at his request. We sat in his office talking and looking out on a great throng of men gathered in the street below, drawn there in the hope that they might be able to obtain employment at the hitherto unheard-of rate of pay. On many previous occasions he had talked over with me his desire to share in some practical manner his prosperity with his employees. As we sat there that morning he spoke at length of his plans and purposes and of the motives back of them. I asked him why he had fixed upon five dollars as the minimum pay for unskilled labor. His reply was,

> Because that is about the least a man with a family can live on in these days. We have been looking into the housing and home conditions of our employees and we find that the skilled man is able to provide for his family, not only the necessities, but some of the luxuries of life. He is able to educate his children, to rear them in a decent home in a desirable neighborhood. But with the unskilled man it is different. He's not getting enough. He isn't getting all that's coming to him. And we must not forget that he is just as necessary to industry as the skilled man. Take the sweeper out of the shop and it would become in a short time an unfit place in which to work. We can't get along without him. And we have no right to take advantage of him because he must sell his labor in an open market. We must not pay him a wage on which he cannot possibly maintain himself and his family under proper physical and moral conditions just because he is not in a position to demand more.

"But suppose the earnings of a business are so small that it cannot afford to pay that which, in your opinion, is a living wage; what then?" I asked.

> Then there is something wrong with the man who is trying to run the business. He may be honest. He may mean to do the square thing. But clearly he isn't competent to conduct a business for himself, for a man who cannot make a business pay a living wage to his employees has no right to be in business. He should be working for someone who knows how to do things. On the other hand, a man who can pay a living wage and refuses to do so is simply storing up trouble for himself and others. By underpaying men we are bringing on a generation of children undernourished and under-developed morally as well as physically; we are breeding a generation of

workingmen weak in body and in mind, and for that reason bound to prove inefficient when they come to take their places in industry. Industry will, therefore, pay the bill in the end. In my opinion it is better to pay as we go along and save the interest on the bill, to say nothing of being human in industrial relations. For this reason we have arranged to distribute a fair portion of the profits of the company in such a way that the bulk of them will go to the man who needs them most.

*　　*　　*

Two years later I was asked to take charge of the Sociological Department. With practically unlimited means and opportunities for carrying on the work at my disposal, and with Mr. Ford deeply interested in it, as he was at that time, it seemed to me an unusual chance for service in a field into which I had always longed to enter, but into which I had never been permitted to go.

"We want to make men in this factory as well as automobiles," is the way Mr. Ford put the matter to me at that time.

This company has outlived its usefulness as a money-making concern, unless we can do some good with the money. I do not believe in charity, but I do believe in the regenerating power of work in men's lives, when the work they do is given a just return. I believe that the only charity worthwhile is the kind that helps a man to help himself. And I believe that I can do the world no greater service than to create more work for more men at larger pay. I can foresee the time when we will have a hundred thousand men—and more—employed in this industry, and I want the whole organization dominated by a just, generous and humane policy.

Such were some of the ideas and ideals of Henry Ford in the years 1914–1915. In accepting the position he offered me I did not think of myself as entering the employ of an impersonal thing called a corporation, but as working with a man whom I had known for many years and for whom I had an unbounded admiration.

I resigned from the Ford Motor Company in 1921. The old group of executives, who at times set justice and humanity above profits and production, were gone. With them so it seemed to me, had gone an era of cooperation and good will in the company. There came to the front men whose theory was that men are more profitable to an industry when driven than led, that fear is a greater incentive to work than loyalty.

The old, humane policies were still professed, but the new influence which had gained the ascendency made impossible, so far as I was concerned, an honest and consistent application of those policies. "Loyalty and good will on the part of the employees toward the company were discounted. Men worked for money," I was informed. "Pay them well, and then see to it that you get your money's worth out of them," seemed to be the new policy of the company.

*   *   *

As in every other man, there is in Henry Ford the mingling of opposing elements. In him, however, the contrast between these elements is more pronounced than in the average man. Phenomenal strength of mind in one direction is offset by lamentable weakness in another. Astounding knowledge of and insight into business affairs along certain lines stand out against a boasted ignorance in other matters. Sensational achievements are mingled with equally sensational failures. Faith in his employees and, at times, unlimited generosity toward them are clouded on occasion by what seems to be an utter indifference to the fate and feelings of men in his employ. There seems to be no middle ground in his make-up. There is no unifying spirit in the warring elements of his nature. There is no line discernible, that I have ever been able to detect, that marks the resultant of the opposing forces within him, and to which one may point and say, "This is the general trend of his life."

He has in him the mental and moral qualities of a great character, if only they were properly blended. He is neither erratic nor unbalanced, as some would have us believe. The true explanation of him seems to me to be this: his mind has never been organized (due, perhaps, in large part to the absence of early educational influences) and his moral qualities and impulses, among which are to be found some of the highest and noblest I have ever known grouped in any one man, have never been compounded and blended into a stable, unified character. One of the most extraordinary and outstanding facts in regard to him, the inexplicable and ironical contradiction, is that a genius in the use of methods for the assembly of the parts of a machine, he has failed to appreciate the supreme importance of the proper assembly, adjustment and balance of the parts of the mental and moral machine within himself. He has in him the makings of a great man, the parts lying about in more or less disorder. If only Henry Ford were properly assembled! If only he would do in himself that which he has done in his factory!

There are times when I felt that the balance had been struck, when the warring elements in his nature had come finally to rest, the blend hoped for had been attained, and then the fires slumbering in him have broken forth with volcanic suddenness and fury, and regrettable qualities have come to the surface. In character he persists in remaining a mixture which defies classification, and in that respect at least, resembles a certain order of genius.

In spite of these displays of contradictory sides of character one never ceases to hope that some day, under heat and pressure of some kind, these mental and moral forces will be fused and blended into one great personality. If only the proper mixture were to be attained and held. If only the scales would cease their endless oscillation, Henry Ford would easily stand out as one of the great characters of this and all time.

"MIRACLE MAKER" [3]

The impact of Henry Ford at the height of his success is strikingly illustrated by this article. John R. Commons was neither a publicity agent nor a writer aiming for a dramatic story. He was an outstanding and respected economist with a special interest in labor. It is therefore all the more impressive that in 1920 he should have hailed Ford as a "miracle maker."

"The industrial miracle of the age," John D. Rockefeller is reported to have said of the Ford Motor Company. He might have added, the psychological miracle of the age. The industrial end is amazing enough. Three completed cars moving off every minute on their own gasoline. The breadwinners of a city of two hundred and fifty thousand at work in one factory.

But the psychological miracle is equally miraculous. Ford reversed the ordinary psychology of industry. Instead of sharing profits with employees at the end of the year he shared them before they were earned. Instead of carefully selecting employees at the gates he takes them as they come— gets a cross section of the community—has a theory that he must carry his share of the maimed, blind, and criminal, because somebody has to do it anyhow—believes in ordinary plain people as they come along.

This is not scientific and is not business. According to the usual ideas Ford ought to break. They tried to prove in court that he was a very ignorant man and could scarcely even read and write. He needs somebody to protect him against himself. And that is what his employees are doing.

Ford says, in effect, to anybody who gets into his works, "How much do you think you are worth?" Well the man thinks he is worth a little more than he has been getting elsewhere. "Why," says Ford, "that's nothing. Here is the biggest thing in the world. We are going to sell a million cars a year and give every family in America a 'Lizzie.' If you get into the

[3] From John R. Commons and others, "Henry Ford, Miracle Maker," *The Independent*, CII, No. 3720 (May 1, 1920), 160–61, 189, which appears to be nonexistent. If there is a known address, please notify Prentice-Hall, Inc., Englewood Cliffs, New Jersey.

game you are worth twice as much, ten times as much, as you have been getting. We will pay you that in advance. Now go to it."

And just the ordinary, everyday man rises up out of himself and sees himself twice as big, ten times as big, as he had ever thought possible. He goes to it.

That is why even men with a prison record have done big things at Ford's. There are 400 of them and the majority making good.

Two thousand men go around with labels, "For light work only." A blind man does the work of three men. The fact is, everybody turns in and protects Ford against himself. He is positively too democratic for this world. One man is just as good as another, he thinks. That certainly is not business. But behold, you see ordinary, common men doing big things at Ford's. . . .

People say, "Oh yes, Ford can do these things because he has such an enormous business. There is nothing at Ford's that can teach other employers anything in any ordinary business subject to competition."

Wrong again. Ford got his enormous business because he did these other things first. Ford is really a plunger—a plunger in social psychology. When he started his profit-sharing scheme in 1914, he had 14,000 employees. He doubled their wages with a bang—that is, he doubled the wages of those who could pass his sociology examination on the clean and wholesome life. In August, 1919, his 14,000 men had become 53,000, and were growing at the rate of 1,200, on an average, a month. The first year after he doubled their wages he made more net profit than he did the year before. . . .

Some people say that the men are "driven" at Ford's. A scientific manager who had come up through machine shops elsewhere had told us he never saw such speeding up. So we looked for it. We had some experience ourselves. The only place where we found it was in some parts of the foundry. There one might say they were speeding up. But those 7,000 foundry workers are nearly all new men. In October, 1918, the foundry had only 700 men. Six thousand farmhands from Europe learning a foundry job might look very active, while 6,000 who have got their pace would look easy. And there were so many of them who were easily at work that the driven ones caught your eye as exceptions.

Anyhow, why shouldn't strong men work hard for eight hours at 75 cents an hour? The Steel Corporation pays the same class of labor 40 cents an hour for twelve hours. One does not like to see them work that hard in the steel mills. And the enormous turnover shows that the steel workers do not keep it up. The foundry is a hard job anyhow—the hardest of all. The turnover there, at Ford's is eight per cent a month, when the average for other shops in the works is four, five, or six per cent. If a foundry turnover, for men who have been employed on the average only six months can be kept down to that figure, at a time when labor was in such demand as it was in the summer of 1919, it would seem that the appearance of overspeeding was not to be taken too seriously. . . .

* * *

That profit-sharing scheme is a curious one. Really that is a wrong name for it. The Ford people now call it "prosperity sharing." That is hardly correct either. It does not depend on the work a man does. It depends on the way he lives outside working hours. It ought to be called a citizenship fund, a community-developing fund, a homemaking's fund. It is fifteen cents an hour devoted to faith in human nature.

It is the payment of a fixed amount to each worker, not a percentage of his wages, nor a prorated distribution of the profits of the concern. It has strings to it, but these strings are different from any ever tied to profit sharing. It does not depend on output, nor upon skill, nor upon length of service. It is based upon the value of the individual in citizenship and in society. It is not based on how much a man brings up the average production of the factory, but upon how much he brings up the average standards of the community, in living, in thrift, in good American citizenship. If he is good in these he may receive today of the profits the company believes he will bring in tomorrow. The idea is that every man wants to be a sober, capable, industrious citizen, and that such a man is the best investment the company can make.

9

Ford in Balance

During the late 1930's the Federal Trade Commission made a detailed study of the motor vehicle industry in order to determine whether its marketing system was such that automobile dealers needed protection against alleged arbitrary practices on the part of the manufacturers. Nothing came of the investigation—although the FTC did conclude that the dealers had valid grievances—but the Commission's report, supported by an elaborate compilation of statistical data, provides a concise and dispassionate narrative of the growth of the principal automobile companies. The excerpts that follow illustrate some salient features of Ford history as seen by a neutral observer.

THE GROWTH OF THE FORD MOTOR COMPANY [1]

Ford's Ideas with Reference to Automobiles

It is said that Henry Ford had certain ideas concerning the proper construction of a "machine" if it were to be practicable for general use in personal transportation. Lightness was one essential—illustrated by the fact that the first "gasoline buggy" weighed about 500 pounds. When the automobile industry was in its early infancy, the general idea seemed to be that an automobile was a luxury vehicle—something that could be afforded only by the wealthy and the very well-to-do, something that would represent an investment of several thousands of dollars in a single unit. It is said that Ford's idea was to construct a motor vehicle that would be so low priced as to be within the means of the great multitude. During the period 1900 to 1910, the general idea seemed to be that after an automobile had been in use approximately two years, there had developed a potential and prospective repair bill of such magnitude that the economical course of procedure was to dispose of the automobile in use and buy a new one. In contrast with this, Ford expressed publicly the idea of building a motor vehicle of such sturdiness that it would have a serviceable life of five years, and of furnishing it to the public at such a low price that, at the

[1] From Federal Trade Commission, *Report on the Motor Vehicle Industry* (Washington, D. C.: Government Printing Office, 1939), pp. 624, 628–31, 632–33, 643–45, 664–66.

conclusion of five years of service, the owner could afford to throw away the worn-out car. An important part of this idea was that of furnishing interchangeable repair parts at prices such that the owner of a Ford car could better afford to buy new replacement parts, when needed, than to have old parts repaired. In short, while other automobile makers expected to supply only a limited demand found among wealthy and very well-to-do people, Ford had the vision of 95 per cent of the population as the source of demand for a low-priced sturdily built motor vehicle . . . .

* * *

Model T was a small, light-weight car, with a 100-inch wheel base and a 56-inch tread, equipped with a 20-horsepower, water-cooled motor with 4-cylinders of 3-3/4-inch diameter and a 4-inch piston stroke, all cast in one block. Originally, it was equipped with a Holly carburetor, a vertical tube radiator, a 10-gallon gasoline tank, and two sets of brakes—one operated by a foot lever acting on the transmission, the other by hand lever acting on the rear axle. The principal distinguishing features were a planetary transmission, a rear axle of unusual design, a magneto built into the flywheel as an integral part of the motor, the use of vanadium steel, and relative lightness and power. Incorporation of the magneto as a part of the flywheel reduced the weight of the car. Vanadium steel was used in the car to make it stronger and lighter, increasing the ratio of the horse-power to the weight and making the car cheaper to operate. The car was simple of design, making it easy to operate and easy to maintain and repair. The parts were so precisely manufactured that a number of cars could be disassembled, the parts mixed, and the same number of cars rebuilt from the parts. It is said that this could not be done with any other car in the low-priced field as late as 1913.

Assembly Plants

Another idea adopted, developed and put into practice by the Ford management was that of decentralization of manufacture, using special-ized plants in the vicinity of Detroit as plants in which to manufacture parts, much of the assembling of these parts into the completed automo-biles taking place in branch assembly plants located in various parts of the United States. Time was required for the purpose of giving full effect to this plan. Eventually, assembly plants were put into operation in the following cities: Kansas City, Missouri, in October 1910; Long Island, New York, in July 1911; Chicago and San Francisco in October 1913; Memphis, Los Angeles, and Denver in November 1913; Detroit and Portland (Oregon) in January 1914; Seattle in February 1914; Cambridge (Massachusetts) and St. Louis in April 1914; Columbus in June 1914;

Dallas and Houston in July 1914; Minneapolis in December 1914; Indianapolis and Pittsburgh in February 1915; Atlanta in March 1915; Cincinnati in April 1915; Cleveland in August 1915; Louisville in October 1915; Buffalo during November 1915; and Milwaukee, Washington, Oklahoma City, and Omaha at dates not specified but not earlier than 1915.

Parts were manufactured in the factories in the vicinity of Detroit or were purchased from factories located at other points, were shipped to these assembly points and were there assembled into the completed automobiles. Several economies are claimed for this system of branch assembly plants. Transportation costs were economized by shipping parts instead of completed automobiles to these assembly plants because the freight cars could be more heavily laden, the straight carloads of parts took lower class rates, and ordinary freight cars could be used instead of special cars. Loading and handling costs were minimized; and diversion and reconsignment were made more practicable and available. Parts made by other manufacturers could be shipped directly to the assembly plants instead of to Detroit; thereby minimizing the freight charges and handling costs. Another advantage was that stocks of parts could be accumulated at the various assembly plants, economizing storage space at the Detroit factories and permitting production of the parts in those portions of the year in which business was slow, thus eliminating the sharp curves of production. The assembly plants also established immediate sources of supply in the regions in which they were located. Dealers were furnished with stocks of parts from these assembly plants; and in many cases were able to drive the cars from the assembly plants to their places of business instead of having them transported by rail.

Also with the establishment of these branches, supervision of dealers was taken over by branch managers. It is said that very close supervision was maintained over the dealer, the control extending even to the appearance of the dealers' salesrooms. Dealers were also required to carry adequate stocks of those parts that were most in demand, thus enabling prompt service and prompt repairs to the car owners.

*   *   *

Price Policy and Prices of Model T Cars

As before stated, the policy of Ford Motor Co. was to manufacture a car of such design and in such manner that it could be offered to the public at a low price and also to reduce prices in line with reduced costs as production economies were achieved through improvement in the structure of the product and in processes of manufacture and through attained volume. Table 60 shows the prices, f.o.b. Detroit, of the model T runabout and the model T touring car as of various dates from October 1, 1908, to February 11, 1926.

Table 60 *Prices of model T runabouts and touring cars, by dates, Oct. 1, 1908, to Feb. 11, 1926* *

Date	Runabout	Touring	Date	Runabout	Touring
Oct. 1, 1908	$—	$850	Aug. 16, 1918	$500	$525
Oct. 1, 1909	—	950	Mar. 4, 1920	550	575
Oct. 1, 1910	—	780	Sept. 22, 1920	395	440
Oct. 1, 1911	590	690	June 7, 1921	370	415
Oct. 1, 1912	525	600	Sept. 2, 1921	325	355
Aug. 1, 1913	500	550	Sept. 16, 1922	319	348
Aug. 1, 1914	440	490	Oct. 17, 1922	269	298
Aug. 1, 1915	390	440	Oct. 2, 1923	265	295
Aug. 1, 1916	345	360	Dec. 2, 1924	260	290
Feb. 21, 1918	435	450	Feb. 11, 1926	290	310

* U. S. Board of Tax Appeals Reports, XI, 1116.

It will be observed from the foregoing table that the price of the touring car on October 1, 1908, was $850, and that it was increased to $950 on October 1, 1909. From that date there was a progressive reduction of the price of this car until it reached a low of $360 on August 1, 1916. During the period of rising wage rates and prices of materials in the latter part of the war period and the immediate postwar period, the prices were increased from time to time to a maximum of $575 on March 4, 1920. After that date, prices were again reduced progressively and reached a new low of $290 on December 2, 1924. There was an increase of $20 on February 11, 1926. Commencing with a price of $590 on October 1, 1911, the prices of the runabout followed a course paralleling that of the prices of the touring car. A minimum of $345 was reached on August 1, 1916, after which the prices were increased progressively to $550 on March 4, 1920, and again were progressively decreased thereafter to a new low of $260 on December 2, 1924. The price of the runabout was increased $30 on February 11, 1926.

With these progressively diminishing prices, the sales of model T cars increased by leaps and bounds. The aggregate sales during the calendar year 1908 amounted to 5,986 cars. The sales during the succeeding calendar years up to 1919 were as follows: 1909, 12,292 cars; 1910, 19,293 cars; 1911, 40,402 cars; 1912, 78,611 cars; 1913, 182,809 cars; 1914, 260,720 cars; 1915, 355,276 cars; 1916, 577,036 cars; 1917, 802,771 cars; 1918, 402,908 cars; and 1919, 777,694 cars.

> *One of the most disputed incidents of Henry Ford's business career was his acquisition of the Lincoln Motor Company. This company was the creation of Henry M. Leland, one of the great pioneers of the American automobile industry. He founded the Cadillac Motor Car Company in 1904 and did much to promote rigorous standards of precision in automobile manufacturing. When the Lincoln company failed, there was much publicity about Ford helping out an old friend. Henry Leland and his son Wilfred believed that they were to be left in charge and their stockholders repaid. Ford, however, took over the Lincoln operation and denied any obligation to its stockholders. The purchase of the Lincoln Motor Company was a marked deviation from Ford's policy of concentrating on a single model; there is some reason to believe that it was Edsel's idea.*

There have been three successive companies named Lincoln Motor Company. The original company was organized on August 29, 1917, by H. M. Leland and associates for the purpose of manufacturing Liberty motors for the United States Government during the World War; and it was incorporated in Michigan. At the conclusion of the war, Lincoln Motor Company had the problem of finding a means of continuing its business. On January 19, 1920, this business was reincorporated in Delaware. The first Lincoln cars were produced in 1920; and all of the funds obtained by selling stock had been put into machinery, tools, and dies. During the depression that set in in the middle of 1920 and continued through 1921, the dealers canceled their purchase orders with this company, its business collapsed, and it could not pay its creditors.

Detroit Trust Company was appointed receiver for Lincoln Motor Company on November 8, 1921; and it continued operating the property until February 4, 1922. On that date all of the property and assets of Lincoln Motor Company were sold to Harold H. Emmons, attorney and agent for Ford Motor Company, for $8,000,000 in cash, subject to land contracts payable amounting to $237,280 and to certain accounts payable for materials and unpaid pay rolls. The receiver paid all taxes, mortgage bonds and expenses of the receivership.

In addition to paying $8,000,000 in cash for the property and assets of this business, Henry Ford arranged for the payment in full of all proper creditors' claims. The receiver paid 47-1/2 per cent of the creditors' claims; and the new Lincoln Motor Company (Michigan) paid the remainder. These payments included reimbursement to H. M. Leland

and certain associates for their liability as endorsers of notes of the old Lincoln Motor Company.

Lincoln Motor Company, a Michigan corporation, was organized in 1922, to acquire from the receiver the assets of the old Lincoln Motor Company of Delaware. Ford Motor Company advanced the $8,000,000 with which to purchase the property and assets at the receiver's sale; and it also made additional payments to the creditors and stockholders amounting to $3,655,699.21, as arranged by Henry Ford. The total of $11,655,699.21 was charged on the books of Ford Motor Co. to an open account with Lincoln Motor Co. of Michigan. The latter issued its common stock in the amount of $11,291,700 in part payment of this account.

Henry M. and Wilfred C. Leland, founders of the original Lincoln Motor enterprise, were assigned important positions in the executive organization of the new Lincoln Motor Co. Shortly thereafter they were ousted from these positions, following which Wilfred C. Leland, who apparently had understood his position to be permanent, and about 2,000 stockholders of the old Lincoln Motor Co. filed a bill in equity asking that the Fords be required to fulfill certain of the terms of an alleged oral agreement entered into prior to the receiver's sale. Leland alleged that on November 21, 1921, two weeks after the receivership and more than two months before the receiver's sale of the assets took place, he had contacted the Fords and had made a satisfactory agreement with them whereby, in consideration for receiving the business as a going concern with the manufacturing and sales personnel intact and retention by the Lelands of important positions in the business after the sale, and in further consideration of the Lelands' refraining from interesting other capital in the sale of the assets of the business at the impending receiver's sale, the Fords agreed to purchase the property at the receiver's sale, paying a price reasonable and fair, to pay all the creditors, and to refund to holders of a certain class of stock the amount invested by them ($1,500,000), and to pay the holders of the remaining class of stock, except such stock as might be in the hands of brokers and held by other persons who had bought the same at $3 or less per share, the full amount of their investment in the stock; that the contracting parties communicated information as to this arrangement to the Federal judge in whose court the sale was to be ordered, that no further efforts were made to interest other capital, and that the sale was held pursuant to the arrangement, the Fords purchasing the tangible assets for $8,000,000.

In a motion to dismiss, the Fords maintained that the oral argument was invalid and unenforceable because against public policy in that it was made for the Lelands especially and only a part of the stockholders and excluded other stockholders from its benefits; that it was within the statute of frauds in that the defendants' promise, if made, was one to answer for the debt, default, or misdoings of another; and that it was a contract to stifle bidding at a judicial sale.

The Supreme Court of Michigan held that the contract was not within the statute of frauds since the alleged promise by the Fords to pay the stockholders was a direct promise and not conditioned upon the promise of another; that the contract apparently was not void on the grounds that it stifled competition in instances where large sums were necessary to purchase assets at a receiver's sale, it is often necessary that preliminary negotiations be entered into in order that the large sums of money be raised. The court found, however, that since the Lelands had publicly announced that they were representing the interests of the stockholders and had apparently represented the interests of a part only, that the oral contract was void, unless an amended bill would show facts not brought out in the original bill. The court also stated that an agreement by the director of a corporation to keep another person permanently in place as officer of such corporation is void as against public policy even though there was not to be any direct gain by the promisor. An amended bill failed to cure the defects; and the contract was recognized as one void and unenforceable because against public policy and because it constituted a fraud upon the rights of third parties; and the parties were left by the court as it found them, neither party having the right to receive affirmative action from a court of equity.

*   *   *

Introduction

In the discussion of the consolidated balance sheets of Ford Motor Co. and its subsidiaries, presented in section 3 of this chapter, it was shown that the principal, if not the only, source of borrowed funds employed in the business of the company consisted of the employees' investment. This is one feature in the company's policy and practice with reference to its employees; and it brings up the subject of wage and personnel policies and practices of the Ford management. It is said that this feature and the other features of the personnel policy and practices of the company are the result, in part, of Henry Ford's experience as an employee before he went into the business of manufacturing automobiles.

Employees' Investment

Important features of the Ford investment plan are as follows: The plan, according to the company's statement, was created for the benefit of Ford employees. The company's policy is to supply complete information concerning the plan to all employees who are interested, but not to solicit employees for investments. Each employee, except those hired temporarily, has the privilege of making investments, or deposits, under the plan, but this is entirely optional with the employee.

The operation of the investment plan is similar to the operation of savings accounts in a savings bank. The investment payments, or deposits, may be made by the employee only out of wages or salary received from the company. Money received by the employee as guaranteed interest on the investment, or as a special return thereon, or as a special bonus of any kind, or received from any outside source, may not be invested under this plan. Employees are allowed to make investment payments not to exceed one-fourth of the wages or salaries received each pay day. Payments, or deposits, are permitted to be made on pay day or either of the two working days immediately following pay day, although, if an employee is absent during such period for reasons that the company believes is beyond the employee's control, the time for making deposits may be extended. No return is allowed on deposits in excess of these limits.

Interest and special returns are paid on all fully paid-up amounts of $50, or multiples thereof, from the date the items are deposited to, but not including, the day on which they are refunded. A return is guaranteed at the rate of 4-1/2 per cent per annum. In addition to the guaranteed return, special returns may be made by action of the board of directors; and these special returns are considered as additional compensations to the employees for services rendered. These guaranteed and these special returns, if any, are paid to the employees on items of $50 standing to the credit of the employee, and they are computed and paid semiannually for the periods beginning January 1 and July 1, respectively, and ending June 30 and December 31, respectively. Items of $50, or multiples thereof, that were refunded between the dates of the regular semiannual payment periods are not included in the computation of any special return that is authorized for the period but draw only the guaranteed return for the length of time within the period that they were invested.

The company reserves the right to require 30 days' notice in writing of an employee's intention to withdraw investments, but this rule is not invoked during a specific period unless ordered by the head office. Subject to this reservation, an employee may withdraw any invested money at any time.

The rules of the company state that at the time employees are given leaves of absence, or laid off for reasons beyond their control, careful consideration is to be given to ascertain whether the employees are expected to return to work shortly. If it is felt that they will return to work within 90 days, their investment accounts may be allowed to stand and to draw the guaranteed return, together with any special return authorized during the 90-day period. If it is decided at any time before the 90 days have

elapsed that the individual's services will not be required at the end of
90 days, the investment account is to be closed out immediately. If the
employee has not returned to work at the end of 90 days, the investment
account becomes payable. However, in the event of unusual circumstances, such as prolonged illness, exception will be made to this general
rule. When employment is terminated, the entire amount invested, with
the accrued return thereon, becomes payable immediately; and from the
date of termination of employment the investment ceases to participate
in any subsequent guaranteed or special return. If an investment account
has been refunded for any reason the amount withdrawn cannot be
redeposited. However, the employee may begin again as a new investor.

In the case of a deceased employee with an investment account of not
more than $100, the amount of the investment may be paid to the em-
ployee's widow; or if he leaves no widow or children, the investment may
be paid jointly to the father and mother or the surviving parent. In case
of a deceased employee with an investment in excess of $100, the invest-
ment is paid, with the accrued return, to the administrator of the deceased
employee's estate or to the executor of his will, upon presentation of a duly
certified copy of authority from the court having jurisdiction in probate
matters.

THE AUTOMOBILE—AND ALOOFNESS [2]

*While the Federal Trade Commission was exploring possible restrictive
practices in the marketing phase of the automobile business, the monopoly-
hunting Temporary National Economic Committee (*TNEC*) was investigating
other aspects. Because the *TNEC* considered the patent system to be an important contributor to the creation of monopolistic conditions, it found itself in the
anomalous position for a predominantly pro-New Deal body of having to cite
Henry Ford as an example to be admired. Elsewhere in the monograph excerpted
here the Committee notes, "The attitude on patents is but a single manifestation
of a pioneer individualism. Ford has been antiunion and has had repeated
battles with the National Labor Relations Board. He was violently opposed
to the National Recovery Administration; is set against 'paternalism,' and has
not hesitated to challenge statutes of various kinds which are expressions of the
public control of business" (p. 121n.). Nevertheless, the fact remained that
Henry Ford disliked patents and so did the* TNEC.

[2] From Temporary National Economic Committee, Monograph No. 31, "Patents
and Free Enterprise," Senate Committee Print, 76th Congress, 3rd Session (Washington, D. C.: Government Printing Office, 1941), pp. 115–19. [This monograph was the
work of Walton H. Hamilton, economist, legal scholar, and at this time one of the
country's leading authorities on prices and monopolies—ed.]

In a sense the automobile has been patented 175,000 times, yet a relative peace prevails along the technological front. One-fifth of all applications for patents have to do with some part of the mechanism for keeping the motorcar going. Nowhere does the network of overlapping claims, all nominally legal, more vividly invite stalemate and litigation; nowhere has the system sown in more fertile ground the seeds of its own destruction. Yet for a quarter century a kind of truce, not without overtones of suspicion, has prevailed along the corporate frontiers of the industry. And the arts which converge in production have developed without the great to-do which attends the clash of private claims.

The quiet has been due to an attitude which is at once nonchalant and practical. It is an expression in commonsense of a free enterprise which in less than a generation converted a luxury into a necessity; which, as a latter day miracle, wove the motorcar into the very fabric of American culture and made its use an aspect of everyday life. The policy dates from a declaration of independence by an upstart, who had won a modest acclaim as a racer, was intent upon making and vending his own car, and refused to pay tribute to an overlord who claimed the technical province as his own. For a lawyer turned engineer had a patent on the whole automobile, and insisted that legally the right to produce was at his pleasure. The "legitimate" trade consisted of firms which possessed his licenses, whose security was constantly threatened by the fly-by-nights. By the owner of the Selden patent Henry Ford was firmly told that he was a poor risk; that as a person he was unfit for the responsibilities of manufacture; that his flivvers were a disgrace to the dirt roads upon which they ran. The purchaser of one of his not-yet-tin-lizzies was threatened with a suit as a contributory infringer of the patent on the internal combustion engine. In those days—near yet far off—a corporate estate sought to be established; litigation raged along the frontiers of the closed industry; Henry Ford discovered patent rights to be an obstacle to personal initiative.

If he had been good at books, Henry Ford would doubtless have called himself an individualist; nor would he have resented the epithet "rugged." He knew, or thought he knew, his modest destiny; he wanted to exercise his right to practice the trade of his choice; he was not going to be stopped by a stranger who waved letters from the Patent Office. He would not accept the credentials at face value; he felt sure they could not survive judicial scrutiny. For as long ago as 1879, one G. B. Selden, a patent lawyer of Rochester, N. Y., applied for the basic automobile patent. His claims comprehended the whole motorcar—all complete with parts, apparatus, mechanism, gadgets. It was a self-propelled vehicle comprising steering wheel, a liquid hydrocarbon engine of the compression type with the engine running at a speed greater than the driven wheels, a disconnecting means between the two, and a body adapted to either persons or goods. In effect, these were rather broad claims, written in terms of technical categories rather than specific devices. As steam, compressed air, electricity fell by the wayside as sources of power, and the internal combustion engine gained the victory, the enveloping claims covered any motor driven by gasoline. With a patience born of shrewdness, Selden did not urge unseemly haste upon the Office. He was, with an occasional amendment of his petition, content to let it lie for 16 years. And not until 1895 was his patent granted.

From early days the rising industry was troubled with squatters. On November 4, 1899—4 years after the patent was issued—Selden granted an exclusive license to the Electric Vehicle Co. It promptly asserted its rights, and, with a vigor greater than it put into its product, it brought suits for infringement against unauthorized manufacturers, their dealers, and their customers. An action, the outcome of which for a time promised to be decisive, was in 1900 lodged against the Winton Motor Carriage Co. After 3 years of skirmishes, which fell short of any general engagement, the Winton Co. acknowledged the validity of the Selden patent and acquired a license to manufacture thereunder. In a short time 16 other leading manufacturers threw up their defense, recognized the patent, and took out licenses.

They joined with 13 other concerns which had already been licensed to form the Association of Licensed Automobile Manufacturers, which promptly embarked on a campagn to terrorize the independents by enforcing to the limit the claims of the Selden patent. A levy of 1-1/4 per cent of the catalog price was enforced upon the members; the fund thus raised served the double purpose of policing the grant and paying the royalties which were its due. The right to license had come to be vested in the Electric Vehicle Co., whose instrument the association was;* its committee was allowed to determine to what new concerns the company's license was to be granted. The right to the trade was now in the hands of those with whom the newcomer must compete. In a word, so far as the licensee could exercise his authority, the industry was closed.

The spirit of enterprise, however, was not yet balked. A united front was to be met by a united front; and, in 1905, 19 concerns which had asked no one's leave to make and market, founded the American Motor Car Manufacturers Association. Although the usual professions of benevolence, mutuality, and good works were put forward, its real purpose—as every member understood—was a concerted defense against the "legitimate" industry. A long series of legal controversies between licensees and tres-

---

* [This is not so. The Electric Vehicle Co. did not control the A.L.A.M.—ed.]

passers ensued; and on September 19, 1909, the Federal court for the southern district of New York upheld the validity of the Selden patent.[3] As a result the organization of independents dwindled to its end in the following year. But a very determined member, Henry Ford, refused to accept the decision and appealed. In 1911, in a radical decision almost unprecedented in its industrial effects, the Circuit Court of Appeals held the Selden patent was to be sharply restricted and that Ford was not an infringer.[4] An industry never tightly locked against the newcomer was thus formally thrown open.

Thus a distrust of patents was engendered; and the circumstances of an industry just off to a dominant place in the economy drove it home. The bumptious persons who had forced their way in were none too respectful of privilege; they had scored a triumph over vested interest; their experience was easily distilled into an attitude toward the whole system. They wanted to drive ahead hard and patent litigation moved at a pace far too slow for their purposes. Their scanty capital did not permit manufacture in the ordinary sense; they had to limit their operations to putting parts together; and the assembly line is not a vantage point from which to contemplate the virtues of an inaccessible technology. Patents came into play, not so much in Detroit, South Bend, Flint, as in places where the components of the automobile were made, and there they were seen as a hazard to production. The price of the motorcar had to be brought down, its market enlarged, its use brought to lower and lower income groups, to the good end that volume be kept up, unit cost be kept down, and the stream of outward bound cars be kept moving. A scrupulous observance of patent protection was a ceremonial for which the industry could find scant time.[5]

Out of experience, policy is born; and a chapter of history lives today in the usages of the Ford Motor Co. The concern applies for patents on its inventions; it must do so, or else it would leave its technical frontiers exposed to raid or even to invasion. But it treats its industrial arts as if

[3] *Electric Vehicle Co. v. Duerr*, 172 F. 923 (1909).

[4] *Columbia Motor Car Co. v. Duerr*, 184 F. 893 (1911). It is a little surprising to find the conflict terminating so abruptly. Suit might have been filed in another jurisdiction, and if another circuit court could have been persuaded to sustain the patent, an appeal might have been taken to the Supreme Court. The contrast with the Bell patents is startling; one judgment closed an industry, the other opened an industry. Yet it is difficult to discover criteria in terms of which the decisions went different ways. A resort to practical standards is more useful; the telephone, far more obviously than the automobile, invites a unified operation.

[5] For a graphic account of the conditions under which the industry got its start, and which early got written into its habits and structure, see Mark Adams, "The Automobile—A Luxury Becomes a Necessity," in Walton Hamilton and others, *Price and Price Policies* (1938), pp. 27–81.

they were common knowledge and makes no use of them as counters in the competitive game. Licenses are freely granted to all responsible parties[6] who can turn the techniques to practical account and no royalties are demanded. Its letters patent are held in reserve as a defense against attack; they are never employed in aggressive warfare. Since parts are purchased and assembled, a large number of suppliers are bound to Ford by contract. The manufacturers of parts are encouraged to develop new methods and to improve their products. But in his agreements with them, royalties are not to be accounted an expense of production. No inventor, or his assignee, is permitted to sit back and claim a return for effort which has become sterile. Ford clings to the maxim that every man must be up and doing; and he yields no place to a person whose concern has come to be the exploitation of his product rather than the improvement of his process. Even today the structure of the industry accords little with the kind of blueprints which investment bankers draw;[7] its trim lines are not overly blurred by a superimposed structure of privilege.

Ford has allowed 92 of his patents to be used by others. In turn he has made use of 515 patents which were not his own. Although the ritual of the license has been duly fulfilled, no money has passed for value received and the frontier has been freely open to the passage of useful knowledge. The company has not escaped litigation; from 1926 to 1938 some 350 threats of suit for infringement have come in; and of these some 60 have materialized as actions in court. But, in spite of its disregard of the prevailing mores, Ford has not done badly. For the period it has lost only one suit in a court of last resort. The flood of threats is a vivid illustration of the dangers which attend business enterprise in a domain where the industrial arts are susceptible to rapid advance. The policy seems to have served the company—and the public—well. There is no evidence that the progress of technology has not been as rapid as in kindred fields where grants have been fully exploited.

The policy of Ford has spread to the industry. A trade association, composed of most of the remainder of the industry, was formed—for cooperation, to keep the industry open, and against private property in the industrial arts.[8] From the first it was agreed that patents were to go into a

---

[6] One wonders if Ford is setting up a standard of financial respectability which initially he himself was unable to meet. In an unsuccessful attempt to liquidate the case of *U. S. v. Hartford Empire* (No. 4426 D. C. N. D. Ohio), by consent decree, it is said that the defendant offered freely to license all "responsible" parties and that Thurman Arnold, Assistant Attorney General in charge of the Antitrust Division, having in mind Ford and the Selden patent, refused.

[7] In the notorious case of the reorganization of Dodge Bros., the industry has had experience of investment control. In a competitive market the reorganized company could not support the inflated capital structure and Chrysler had to take over.

[8] After some eight changes in name, it is now known as the Automobile Manufacturers' Association.

pool upon which all might freely draw and that no royalties were to be paid. To this end a cross-licensing agreement was executed by almost all the members. Ford, who had fought the court fight alone, held formally aloof, although in practice he went along. Packard which held patents which it did not wish to share became a fellow traveler, cooperated with the Association, was given access to the inventions in the pool, and was charged for the privilege.

FORD IN THE HISTORY OF TECHNOLOGY [9]

This selection is included here because it was written during Ford's lifetime although published after his death. The author, a Swiss scholar, is one of the great historians of technology. Here he discusses the analogies between Ford's ideas on production and wages and the development of scientific management at the end of the nineteenth century. In addition he undertakes to show Ford's work as a logical stage in the history of mechanized production.

To realize his conviction that the automobile must become a people's vehicle Henry Ford employs the means and the ideas of his time. He uses them like building-stones, often with fresh meaning, and simplifying them wherever possible. The assembly line supplants Taylor's* motion studies and the yet more complex fatigue studies of his successors. The interchangeability of parts, already known in the field of agricultural machinery in the sixties for maintenance of the reaper, takes on another nuance in Ford's hands. He stresses its usefulness for the automobile: "The machinery of today, especially that which is used in general life away from the machine shop, has to have its parts absolutely interchangeable, so that it can be repaired by nonskilled men." [10]

He follows Taylor's method, unusual for the time, of so far as possible reducing working hours and raising wages. Here too the foreman retains his function. But when Taylor, in his famous experiments on shoveling, tells his laborers in the yard of the Bethlehem Steel Company: "Pete and Mike, you fellows understand your job all right, both of you fellows are first class men, but we want to pay you double wages," [11] he still is set upon raising production within the factory. Henry Ford goes further, and regards low wages as "the cutting of buying power and the curtail-

---

[9] From Siegfried Giedion, *Mechanization Takes Command* (New York: Oxford University Press, Inc., 1948), pp. 116–17. Copyright © 1948 by Oxford University Press, Inc. Reprinted by permission of the publisher.
* [Frederick Winslow Taylor, the founder of scientific management—ed.]
[10] Henry Ford, *Moving Forward* (New York, 1930), p. 128.
[11] F. B. Copley, *Frederick W. Taylor*, II (New York, 1923), 58.

ment of the home market." [12] Indeed Henry Ford views production and
sales as a unit and, long before the high-pressure salesmanship of the
1930's, builds a world-wide organization to distribute his products. The
efficiency of the sales force is as precisely worked out as the tempo of the
assembly line.

A further broadening of the circle might take up the question: How has
the automobile affected living habits? In what measure has it stimulated
and in what measure has it destroyed? How far, then, is its production
to be encouraged and to what extent curbed?

As a phenomenon, Henry Ford crystallizes anew the independent
pioneering spirit of 1830 and 1860. In a period of elaborate banking and
credit institutions, a period governed by the stock exchange, when the
lawyers are needed at every move, Henry Ford trusts none of them and
operates without banks.

In an age when anonymous corporations grow to giant proportions, he
would exercise patriarchal power over his worker force, like a master over
his journeymen. He would be independent of everyone in everything. He
gathers in his own hands forests, iron and coal mines, smelting furnaces,
rubber plantations, and other raw materials.

But just as great cities become increasingly ungovernable when they
overgrow themselves, great industrial concentrations elude the patriarchal
hand when they develop to the gigantic.

Ford did not have to spend his life, like Oliver Evans,* furthering
ideas ungrasped by his contemporaries. He may have had the same
indomitable energy; but he also had the advantage of coming not at the
start, but at the end of the mechanistic phase. Success does not depend
on genius or energy alone, but on the extent to which one's contemporaries
have been prepared by what has gone before.

The assembly line too, as conceived by Henry Ford, forms in many ways
the fruition of a long development.

[12] Henry Ford, *My Life and Work* (Garden City, 1923–27), chapter on wages.

* [Oliver Evans, inventive genius, built a continuous-process gristmill in Pennsylvania in 1787 and a steam-powered vehicle in 1805—ed.]

10

Ford in Decline

The coming of the Great Depression brought disillusionment. An industrial system that had promised so much appeared to be in complete collapse, and the prophets of the new era of machine-produced plenty, of whom Henry Ford had been the foremost, were discredited. The mood is reflected by Jonathan N. Leonard, a journalist writing when depression conditions were at their worst. Henry Ford's achievements no longer mattered; instead, the emphasis shifted to his faults and his blunders. Yet for all his cynicism, Leonard could not avoid liking Ford as a man.

"ONLY THE EMOTION OF PITY"[1]

Before he goes any further the author of this book has a confession to make. He started to write in a fine fury of indignation. He had seen the Ford factory, the workmen with their dull eyes, their rapid dull hands, obeying their mechanical drill masters as slavishly as if they were valve-stems yielding to the superior force of the camshaft. He had heard about the horrors of life under the ten-acre roofs of River Rouge. He had heard about Ford's cruelty, his insensitivity, his intolerance, his hatred of everything related to beauty, freedom, human dignity. He had observed his maniacal attacks on the Jews, his destructive contempt for all those regions of human life which lay outside his own narrow experience. He had felt the heat of that hatred toward Ford and all his works which has seared the edges of nearly every human spirit in Detroit. "Surely," he thought, "here is the evil genius of twentieth-century America, a first cause of rusty tin cans, defiant ugliness, prohibition, hypocritical police morality, proud ignorance—all the symptoms of that haloed greed which is the motive power of America's religion of business."

But after he had gone a little more deeply into the fascinating and fantastic story of Henry Ford, he began to feel another emotion. Here was a man, in some ways friendly, simple, kindly. He possessed a billion

[1] From Jonathan Norton Leonard, *The Tragedy of Henry Ford* (New York: G. P. Putnam's Sons, 1932), pp. 11–13, 15–16, 21, 47–48, 113–14, 212–15, 230–31, 235–37, 241, 242.

dollars—more or less—which he had come into partly by accident, partly by ruthlessness, partly by a strange sort of nonrational intelligence. Everything concerned with the gathering and keeping of this vast sum of money was increasingly repellent as the years went by. But somehow it didn't seem to matter. After all, industrial exploitation was nothing new. Ford was no worse than Frick or Gary. The River Rouge was not nearly as bad as the coal mines of West Virginia or the horrible little company villages of the South.

And Henry Ford did not give his entire attention to the conservation and augmentation of this fabulous hoard. Beyond the bristling fences which ring his plants his motives were often benign and good, although certainly not intelligent. He really wanted to use his unprecedented wealth to help humanity, point out the various errors of which he saw it was guilty—smoking cigarettes, for instance, and tolerating that conspirator against mankind, the International Jew. He actually wanted all men to have the happiness which would come from living correctly, and when they refused, he was willing to spend large sums to persuade them.

And what pathetic failure met him at every excursion beyond his factory gates! He was set upon by cranks, fanatics, even criminals. Third-rate politicians fattened upon him. Fourth-rate ministers played upon his simple-minded prejudices. Newspapers exploited his picturesque ignorance. His tabloid literacy put him at the mercy of secretaries who did his reading for him. He was victim of hordes of yes-men who discovered subtly what he wanted to hear and cooked up stories to please him. Time and time again he went sadly back to Detroit, the ridicule of the world ringing in his ears. He would listen to the roar of his huge factory, watch the little black beetles rolling off the assembly line, feel the reassurance of a billion dollars beneath his feet, and sally forth again—only to meet with the same reception. It is easy to forget a number of things about Henry Ford and feel only the emotion of pity.

*   *   *

Beyond the Ford plant lies Detroit, separated by five miles of the most complete ugliness in America. Open country of a few years ago is half built-up with flimsy houses, gas stations, hot dog stands. Lesser factories drool rusty iron among the weeds. In vacant lots the unemployed offer cheap lubricating oil to the passing traffic. If we stop at one of these pathetic stands and mention the name "Ford," we get a blast of invective hot enough to start a prairie fire. If we mention the word to a shopkeeper, we get an unfriendly look and distrustful silence. If we manage to penetrate to the office of a powerful magnate in the center of the city, we get an abrupt refusal to discuss Henry Ford or any of his works. Detroit is a city of hate and fear. And the major focus of that hatred and fear is the astonishing plant on the River Rouge.

But—in the new and costly Public Library on Woodward Avenue there are numerous books praising Ford, explaining how his policies are going to remake the world. Some of them have marginal notes in strange handwriting by people who believe him the second coming of Christ. There is the Ford Hospital, run rigidly like a factory, but marvelously cheap and effective. There are thousands of homes scattered about the city which were built with his liberal wages. On the steppes of Russia the peasants have placed his picture in the icon corner of their hovels beside the picture of Lenin. There have been "Ford for President" movements. Farmers have looked to him for cheap fertilizer, cheap tractors, assured markets.

Around this strange man have centered more worship, more hatred, more perplexity than around any private citizen in history. He is the master of a billion dollars. His feeblest opinions have made the front page of the world press. Whole nations have begged him to buy them body and soul. He is hated by nearly everyone who has worked for him, and at one time was worshipped by nearly everyone who had not. His story is certainly the most fascinating in all the gaudy tale of American business.

We shall try to tell that story, placing the emphasis where it ought to be placed, on Ford's fumbling attempts to rise above the dubious distinction of mere wealth. He failed, often ludicrously, but at least he tried. Which is more than most rich men do.

*　　*　　*

And Ford himself? Some of his early associates are inclined to give him no credit at all. But they are wrong, partially at least. Ford was not wholly human. He was ignorant and intolerant. His confidence in his own ability was unruffled by the doubts which come with knowledge. He was acquisitive without limit and egotistic without deviation. His mind was astonishingly simple. He could concentrate on a single idea almost as perfectly as the inmate of a State Asylum who can remember the number of every car which passes the gate. Such a man is a real asset to a company in the early stages of a chaotic and fumbling industry.

And Ford's single idea was a good one. Whether or not he thought of it first himself is unimportant, for it was Ford who stuck to it through thick and thin. He would build a cheap car for the large public. Every other consideration was out. Not a penny would he spend on appearance, on sport or fashion appeal, on comfort or more than necessary speed. The cars would be alike. They would "get you there and get you back"—nothing more. They would be an expression of Ford's own personality, bare, utilitarian, perverse. They might have their own peculiar weaknesses, but they would not cater to the weaknesses of others. Without exception they would be painted black when they left the factory—a symbol of their standardization in other respects. Every Ford on the roads of America would look like every other. Only the drivers would vary.

*   *   *

No. Ford's pacifism was genuine, and a great deal more logical than most of his ideas. It had something even deeper than logic behind it. It came from his fundamental emotional philosophy. He believed that work, productive work, was absolutely the only thing that mattered in the world. People should live "cleanly" to keep healthy. They would work better if they were healthy. They must live submissively. Machines did the work of the modern world. People should be as much like machines as possible. They must save. If they did not, they would have to be provided for by charity, and charity was a noneconomic thing, an element of confusion in the structure of industry. Ford did not carry this train of reasoning to its logical limits. If he had, it would have led him to Communism, and he was too much of an individualist. Or it would have led him to old-fashioned autocracy, and he hated its cultural connotations—ermine robes and privileged immorality. Fascism had not yet been born—that bare, ugly autocracy. If it had, the Ford of 1915 might have hailed it as the solution of the world's problems.

But there was one thing which definitely did not fit into his philosophy, and that was war. No one has ever been able to accuse Ford of nationalism, or patriotism for that matter. His attitude toward life was typically and narrowly American, as we shall show later, but he did not think of it this way. He believed that his formula of productive work above all else was a universal thing. It would work in India, Ireland, Germany as well as it worked in America. Historical emotions did not affect him. He had not heard of them. What if England did lose control of the seas? Would that stop her from working? What if Germany was being kept from her "place in the sun"? Would that stop the wheels of her factories? What if Serbia were being trampled on? She would probably be more prosperous as part of a large economic unit. The emotions, regrettable but deeply human, which lie behind war meant nothing to Henry Ford. He saw only that war destroyed the machines, the productivity, the regularity which he loved so well.

*   *   *

Ford had other rural American characteristics, but they are rather commonplace. He was an individualist to the point of excessive egotism. He could not work with others, and never did when he could avoid it, getting rid of the early associates who had built up his success as soon as possible. Like so many individualists he would not stand for individualism in others. He was intolerant in almost every respect. If he did not approve of a man, he would have nothing to do with him. Like most homesick country boys, Ford loved the birds and the flowers—one of his more pleasant qualities. He hated even mildly fashionable society and would tolerate no contact with it. He hated abstract learning because it was "non-productive" and because he possessed none of it himself. He hated financiers because they lived in large cities and because he did not understand their operations.

Much has been written about Henry Ford as "the great American enigma." His facial expression has much to do with it. There is something baffling about his smile. And he has a fondness for short, cryptic sentences—a favorite rural method of appearing wise. But there is really nothing hard to understand about Ford. His commentators start at the wrong end. They are dazzled by his wealth and success; they think there must be something remarkable about his character. And when they hear him make a statement not in keeping with his position as an industrial leader, they take refuge in the conclusion that he is an enigma. As a matter of fact all his opinions can be heard around the general store cracker box on any winter afternoon. The remarkable thing about Henry Ford is that he got hold of a billion dollars. Without that golden backing he would never have been taken seriously, for intellectually and philosophically he was fifty years behind the times. But where a billion dollars sits, there is the head of the table.

*   *   *

But for the time being Ford kept his presidential ambitions more or less under his hat. His more immediate concern was the uncompleted Muscle Shoals power plant and nitrate factory* which the government had built during the war at the cost of some $80,000,000 and was now trying to get rid of. Ford had always had a hankering to play with water power, although he had too much sense to try to use it extensively in his industry. Water power is an excellent thing, but it is subject to economic laws like everything else, and it cannot compete with coal except in certain instances. Ford knew this perfectly well and proved that he knew it by keeping his factory at Detroit instead of moving it to Niagara or the Pacific Coast. But when he was talking largely about his dreams for the future, economic laws had not the same authority as they possessed when he was thinking of practical matters. Muscle Shoals fascinated him. The water-power idea would have been enough alone, but the added possibility of manufacturing cheap nitrate fertilizer for his beloved farmers made Ford lean back in his chair and drift off in a fog of extremely shaky statistics.

On July 14, 1921, Ford had made an offer for the nitrate plant and

* [Wilson Dam, on the Tennessee River in Alabama. Now part of the TVA—ed.]

the electric power to run it. There were four propositions, all extremely complicated and detailed, but they boiled down to $5,000,000 in cash and a 100 year lease at $1,500,000 a year. Ford called this buying the plant complete for $150,000,000—which was the total amount to be paid in the ensuing century. The government did not see it that way. There was still $28,000,000 to be spent before the plant was complete, and Ford's $1,500,000 a year was no more than annual interest on this sum alone at a rate a little above five per cent. Secretary Weeks [John W. Weeks, Secretary of War] rejected Ford's offer on July 25, on the technical grounds that the government could not guarantee the 600,000 horsepower which Ford stipulated in his offer.

Ford persevered and renewed his offer in slightly modified form. It went before Congress in January, 1922. No doubt it would have been rejected without debate as vastly too low if another factor had not intervened. We must remember that by this time Ford had decided to be President. He was laying the foundations of his campaign and his first move was an address to the voters which he released to the papers on January 11.

We have observed some of Ford's industrial dreams before this, and we have noticed a curious thing about them. As long as he stuck to the Model T, his feet remained fairly firmly on earth. But when he was thinking of a project which he was unlikely to carry out, he allowed his imagination to run away with him. All his vague ideas and naive prejudices came to the surface in the form of "production" and statistics.

The future which Ford predicted for Muscle Shoals was certainly the wildest dream even he was capable of. To begin with, the three dams strung along the Tennessee River were to become a city seventy-five miles long. Not exactly a city either. Ford did not like cities. This was to be something new—a long line of industries closely in contact with the farms. The workers would not be city people, but virtuous country folks. The valley would become a row of small towns, linked with powerlines, and manufacturing in virtue and sobriety the fertilizers, tractors, and other things necessary to restore America to its original rural simplicity.

So far so good. Such a rural-industrial center if it were possible might very well be a paradise for the working man. But Ford's mind had torn loose from its moorings and was wandering into even more Utopian regions. The power of the Tennessee River, he stated definitely, was sufficient to run all the industries of the country. It was actually only some 600,000 horsepower, as Ford had good reason to know, and this was a minute part of the power used in America. But Ford had dreamed a dream, and there was no stopping him now.

As if a country with all its wheels turned by the Tennessee River were not enough for one day, Ford launched forth on another of his fantasies. If he were given the chance, which he trusted the American people to give him, he would make the country into a completely electrified nation. Every farmer would harness the little brooks and streams which ran through his fields. Electric wires would run along every country lane, and the farmer would never have to leave his home to compete with the corrupt workers of the city.

In making this announcement Ford was probably perfectly sincere. That was the way his mind worked. But the plan turned out to be a masterpiece of demagogy. The hard-pressed farmers, scratching to pay off their mortgages, struggling with the overproduction of agricultural products brought about largely by Ford's tractors, hailed Ford as the Moses who would lead them to the promised land. Even in the hated cities were millions of lost and homesick country people who saw in Ford's electrification project their chance to get back to the simple life they loved. The idea that the whole thing was a hollow dream never occurred to them. Wasn't this Henry Ford the richest man in the world? Didn't he make a hundred thousand automobiles a month? He certainly ought to know what he was talking about.

So they wrote to their Congressmen—pathetic, tearful letters begging them to give Ford the chance he wanted. And when Congress, knowing well enough that Ford could never fulfill his promises, refused after much debate to hand Muscle Shoals over to him for practically nothing, the farmers began to talk of throwing the whole gang out and letting a real industrial genius run the show.

*   *   *

So by 1924 we feel justified in drawing a sketch of what it meant to work for Ford. For this purpose there is no lack of material. Half of Detroit has either worked "at Ford's" or still does, and information abounds. Do not attempt to extract it from a Ford worker. He will suspect you of being a spy. Ask the unemployed or the men who have jobs with some strong company such as the Standard Oil. Gas station attendants are accessible and usually as talkative as barbers. Many of them are ex-Ford men. Mention his name to one of them and if you had any impression that the Ford plant was a paradise for the working man, that impression will disappear in a welter of picturesque epithets which your informant has probably been practicing for years.

We shall not attempt to whitewash any of the other automobile factories in Detroit. They are almost all horrifying and repellent to the last degree. But the Ford factory has the reputation of being by far the worst. Visitors find it hard to believe this, for the four hundred drab creatures who are conducted daily through the plant are kept to a beaten track. First they see the toolmakers—the aristocrats of the automobile world.

They cannot be standardized and they cannot be driven, for their work depends on their individual judgment, and upon their work depends the efficiency of the whole factory. Everything is very clean and neat. But the workers take little pleasure in it, for it means the possibility that they will be punished if they drop an oily rag on the floor. At intervals the visitors pass drinking fountains marked "for visitors only." Let a worker try to drink from one of them and see what happens. The guide next leads them to the glass plant, where the operations are entirely mechanical and almost no men are to be seen. There are several other points of interest which are similarly automatic. The visitors are conducted to each, and it is duly pointed out to them that they, prospective purchasers of Ford cars, will benefit from the small amount of human labor which these machines require.

The final *pièce de résistance* is the famous assembly line, which contrary to the general impression plays a very small part in the manufacture of an automobile. The assembly line system is by no means peculiar to the Ford plant or even to the automobile industry, but the example at the River Rouge is certainly the most spectacular, for it is the apple of Ford's eye, and has been dressed up in various ways. There is hardly an American who has not heard it described a dozen times—how the cars begin at one end as a bare frame and roll off the other end under their own power. The visitor who watches this miracle is so fascinated that he does not take time to observe the men who perform it. In turn the men do not observe the visitors. In most factories they will look around, perhaps hoping to see a pretty girl in the party. But not at Ford's. The line moves inexorably onward. The men have exactly time to perform their minute operation before the work passes out of reach.

*   *   *

Over the whole Ford plant hangs the menace of the "Service Department," the spies and stool pigeons who report every action, every remark, every expression. The men are constantly shifted about so they never learn who they can trust. When a new man comes into a section he is looked at with suspicion and observed carefully. They try little stratagems to test him. One of them will risk his job and ask him a question. If a look of genuine terror comes over his face, he is all right. He's a Ford worker like the rest. But if he answers and tries to draw his questioner away from his work, he is a stool pigeon.

The scope and efficiency of the spy system is incredible. A boy on an errand who has stopped to buy a bar of chocolate will find that he has been spotted. The man who wipes the oil off his machine half a minute before the closing bell meets the same fate. The man who expresses himself carelessly in a private conversation finds that his words have been card-indexed in the office. The man who joins one of the pathetically weak unions which exist feebly in Detroit finds himself transferred to the dreaded foundry. When a man has been called away from his work for a medical examination or some other good reason, he is given a slip of paper stating the exact time he started. This is a passport to get him by the spotters in the factory yard. The chances are that it will be examined carefully before he reaches his destination. When he does arrive, a clerk in the doctor's office calculates the time the trip consumed and checks it against a table of distances.

No one who works for Ford is safe from the spies—from the superintendents down to the poor creature who must clean a certain number of toilets an hour. There are spies who ask embarrassing questions of the visitors' guides, spies who worm their way into labor unions, spies who speak every language under the sun. The system does not stop at the factory gates. An anonymous letter accusing a man of stealing Ford parts is enough to bring him before the "Service Department." He is forced to sign a "Permission for Search" which allows Ford detectives to ransack his home, turn out all his poor possessions in hopes of finding a Ford incandescent lamp or a generator armature. There are spies to watch these in turn.

Nor are the salesmen on the road and the agents in distant cities safe from undercover supervision. If after the manner of salesmen, they have entertained the trade by throwing a party in the roadhouse, they are hailed before the "Ford Court" and punished in direct proportion to the amount of liquor consumed and in inverse proportion to the amount of clothes the entertainers wore on the occasion. If the manager of the French or the Argentine plant goes native, he may be sure that an exact report will find its way back to Detroit.

*   *   *

During the twenty years when the Ford Motor Company was the marvel of the business world, Henry Ford, as we have seen, made many strange excursions outside his factory gates. From every one of these he returned a bewildered and beaten man. But as long as the Model T, his first and only success, continued to sell, he did not become discouraged. A man may be ridiculed, rebuffed, denounced, his ignorance held up before the nation, but as long as his income is thirty or forty million dollars a year, he will continue to fight. That amount of money is a license to push into any field, no matter how unfamiliar.

But with the death of the Model T a great change came over Henry Ford. His formula had finally failed. His self-confidence was based upon his simple-minded belief that he could always "produce" in ever-increasing amounts, and so lead the nation into the glories of the mechanized future. He did not consider himself a mere manufacturer, like the Dodges or Chrysler. He was a prophet with a message for the world. The fact that his message was bare, ugly, tyrannical did not keep people from accepting it as long as he was the most successful industrialist in the country. In the United States a record of commercial success makes a man an authority on every subject.

* * *

After the failure of his formula, Ford became just another manufacturer. The glory was gone. Presently his plant would produce the Model A, which would have a brief success. The newsboys would pay it the unique compliment of folding their papers so that the Ford advertisement formed the front page. But history would repeat itself, and over a shorter cycle. Henry Ford would fall into his old ways, relapse into his old formula. He would refuse to allow the Model A to follow the demands of the public. It would become obsolete in its turn, and presently be passed in sales volume by Chevrolet and approached by that enterprising newcomer, Plymouth.

The Model A cycle ended in 1931. During the summer the Ford plan closed down in preparation for yet another model, scheduled to appear in January, 1932. But we may feel confident that it too will follow the old route, yield to Ford's innate stubborness, and become obsolete in a few years like the Model T and the Model A. And even if the company does manage to persuade its owner to follow the rest of the industry and keep up with engineering and fashion changes, Henry Ford will never be a prophet again. He will merely be a manufacturer, and since the crash of 1929 the American people refuse to worship without reserve the god of mass-production.

THE FORD "RETRACTOR" [2]

The Literary Digest *was a mirror of American opinion during the 1920's. This article, summing up comment on Henry Ford's apology in 1927 for the anti-Semitic articles in the* Dearborn Independent, *reflects an ambivalence in American opinion. At this time Henry Ford was still a demigod, but should a demigod have committed such an indisputable and admitted blunder?*

Henry Ford's abject apology for the publication of "Jew-baiting" articles during the last seven years in his weekly magazine, the *Dearborn*

[2] From *The Literary Digest*, XCIV, No. 4 (July 23, 1927), 8–9, which appears to be nonexistent. If there is a known address, please notify Prentice-Hall, Inc., Englewood Cliffs, New Jersey.

Independent, our Jewish press hails almost unanimously as courageous and manful. "The truth has conquered," exclaims *The Jewish Daily Forward* of Detroit, in an editorial syndicated through a country-wide chain of Jewish newspapers, which continues: "Ford admits frankly before the entire world that he sinned against the Jewish race, and now openly asks forgiveness. More than that we cannot expect." The peak of approval by the vast majority of the press at large may be seen in the Des Moines *Register*, which says: "the retraction, thanks to Ford's remarkable position before the world, is more sensational than the attacks. It takes size to do a grand thing in a grand way."

Mr. Ford's six-hundred-word confession and apology was front-page news in all the principal daily papers in this country, and an amazing amount of editorial space has been given to comment on it. In what contributors to F. P. A.'s * column in the New York *World* cleverly call "the Ford retractor," Mr. Ford declares that "henceforth the *Dearborn Independent* will be conducted under such auspices that articles reflecting upon the Jews will never again appear in its columns." He explains that in the multitude of his activities it was impossible for him to devote personal attention to the publication whose conduct and policy he delegated to men upon whom he relied implicitly. Learning that Jews have come to regard him as a promoter of anti-Semitism and their enemy, he has been making a personal survey of the resented articles, and says:

> I am deeply mortified that this journal, which is intended to be constructive and not destructive, has been made the medium for resurrecting exploded fictions, for giving currency to the so-called Protocols of the Wise Men of Zion, which have been demonstrated, as I learn, to be gross forgeries, and for contending that the Jews have been engaged in a conspiracy to control the capital and the industries of the world, besides laying at their door many offenses against decency, public order, and good morals.
>
> Had I appreciated even the general nature, to say nothing of the details of these utterances, I would have forbidden their circulation without a moment's hesitation . . . .

Mr. Ford's repudiation of anti-Semitism is such news to the press throughout the world that its effect will spread much farther than the foolish attacks which appeared in his own limited publications, the Grand Rapids *Press* points out. "If one of the richest men in the world can't get away with an anti-Semitic movement in this country, nobody else will have the nerve to try it," says the New York *Telegram*, "and for that we can all be thankful, Gentiles as well as Jews." "Mr. Ford is noted for doing unusual and startling things," notes the Brooklyn *Eagle*, "but he has never done anything comparable to this dramatic conscience clearing." The kind of approval exprest [*sic*] in scores of editorials is fairly repre-

* [Franklin P. Adams, well-known literary critic and columnist of the period—ed.]

sented by the Pittsburgh *Gazette Times* in saying "everyone else (save Ford) has known about the articles and the effect of them":

"Not alone Jews have been resentful. They have offended against a cardinal principle of Americanism. But there will be common satisfaction in Mr. Ford's confession of error, and in his promise to sin no more against a great body of American citizens whose worthy contributions to the national welfare are known of all and to which he now testifies."

Among representative Jewish journals, *The American Hebrew*, New York, says editorially that any man who writes such words as those contained in Mr. Ford's confession and retraction "must be accepted as a true repentant; it breathes honesty and sincerity no matter how the cynic may rationalize the motives behind the document. We forgive and will seek to forget."

At the same time *The American Hebrew* publishes an article by E. G. Pipp, a Detroit editor, and the first editor of the *Dearborn Independent*, who says that he resigned rather than take Mr. Ford's orders to publish anti-Jewish articles which appeared later under his successor.

The editor of *The Jewish Tribune*, New York, expresses "profound satisfaction" over Mr. Ford's apology for the terrible mistakes he had made, but suggests further atonement:

"As the world's richest man, Henry Ford has the unique opportunity of making an *amende honorable* to the Jewish people by sponsoring a world-wide campaign of education against national chauvinism, religious bigotry, and racial antagonism."

Wide currency has been given to these words of Julius Rosenwald, the Chicago philanthropist:

"It is never too late to make amends, and I congratulate Mr. Ford that he has at last seen the light. He will find that the spirit of forgiveness is not entirely a Christian virtue."

One of the comparatively few utterly severe critics is the *Chicago Tribune*, which holds Mr. Ford to strict accountability for "his own medium of expression and promotion." The *Dearborn Independent* "existed for him and because of him; he was its authority and payroll." Whereupon the *Tribune* avers:

"There are few things so remorseless as a certain type of good and wealthy man taking to cover from the consequences of error either realized or feared for the future. Mr. Ford advances an empty head to explain his cold feet, and the only plausibility is contained in the fact that it took him until advanced years to discover that Benedict Arnold was not a modern writer, and that the Revolution was not fought in 1812." *

* [This refers to statements Ford made in testimony during his libel suit against the *Tribune*—ed.]

Ford's plea "will be laughed at all over the United States," in the opinion of the *Richmond Times-Dispatch*, which concludes: "If he had felt it necessary, for more or less obvious business reasons growing out of recent developments, to recant and retract and apologize, he would have occupied a far more dignified position if he had merely recanted and retracted and apologized. In denying knowledge of the anti-Semitic policy of his magazine and in disavowing any understanding of its effect on the Jewish people, he has set himself up as a target for further ridicule."

Curiosity concerning how Mr. Ford's retraction came to be made has produced many news column stories, some connected with intimations of settlement of two suits for libel pending against him by Aaron Shapiro, a Jewish organizer of farm cooperatives, and Herman Bernstein, a Jewish journalist; others from financial quarters suggesting pressure of competition from powerful rival automobile making and selling organizations. J. A. Palma, head of the New York field force of the United States Secret Service, who went to see Ford to secure correction of an inaccurate article in which the service was interested, says that Ford took the occasion to say of the anti-Jewish articles that he "wished this thing could be stopt [*sic*] and the wrong righted." Palma volunteered to help, and Ford said: "Go to it." The outcome was the letter of apology sent in duplicate to Louis Marshall, head of the American Jewish Committee, and to Arthur Brisbane * for publication.

Washington correspondents, too, got very busy on stories of the possible rebuzzing of the Presidential bee in Ford's bonnet. Having given his retraction to Arthur Brisbane, of the Hearst newspapers, for publicity through all news agencies, the correspondent of the New York *World* scented a Hearst "dry" boom for Ford, reminding the public of Hearst's opposition to Al Smith and the featuring of Anti-Saloon League criticism of Coolidge in the Hearst press. The New York *Herald Tribune* correspondent found political Washington wondering whether the "Presidential rash undoubtedly affecting Ford" back in 1923–24, had broken out again, but reported that the wiser heads conclude that "the probable motive is found in business affairs." The Chicago *Journal of Commerce* man wired that, despite all business logic as explaining the recantation, "many astute gentlemen in Washington" believe "the real motive is to be found in a renewal of hope," at a time when both Democrats and Republicans are ready to concede that "nothing is apt to stop Coolidge." According to the *Washington Post*, however, "the premise that Ford aspires to the Presidency can be attributed only to the dearth of actual news," and "the conclusion that the Democrats would take his candidacy

* [Columnist and editor of the Hearst papers—ed.]

seriously is the most unkind thrust that has yet been directed at that much-maligned party." An interview by the International News Service circulated just prior to the news of the apology quotes Mr. Ford as saying that Coolidge has made a good President, he favors giving the President a third term, thinks "he'll probably get it anyway." As to personal political ambitions, Ford declared he had none, and never has had.

"OTHER PEOPLE'S MONEY" [3]

When the New Deal arrived, Henry Ford's prestige was still high enough to enable him to defy the government by refusing to accept the automobile code. What weakened this prestige more than anything else was his intransigence toward labor unions and the strong-arm tactics that he permitted Harry Bennett's Security Department to use. This article by John T. Flynn, a well-known writer and newspaper columnist of the day, illustrates the sharp contemporary reaction to the beating of union organizers at the Ford plant on May 26, 1937.

Watch the Ford Myths Go By
—The Pious Art of Mayhem—
So Smash the Tin Lizzie

One of our beloved myths is Henry Ford. He comes at times to be a sort of touchstone by which proposed legislation is tested. If a tax or a regulation or a policy can be shown to be something that might affect Henry Ford it must be bad. If you enact such a law, what will become of Henry Ford? The mere mention of the horrendous possibility that something might happen to Henry Ford is enough to damn any measure.

The basis of this childlike terror is that if there had been no Henry Ford there would be no automobile era, just as there would have been no American electricity era had there been no Samuel Insull.* There is also the other simple assumption that the making of cheap automobiles is entirely the product of the Ford brain and that if Ford stopped, the industry would stop. Of course if Ford's labor stops the industry also stops. As a matter of fact, it is not generally perceived how little any one man contributes to such an industry. For the Ford industry needs, not merely labor and a manager, but the accumulated contributions of

---

* [Utilities magnate who built an enormous and complicated structure of public utility holding companies during the 1920's. It collapsed when the Depression came. Insull was tried for fraud but acquitted—ed.]

[3] From John T. Flynn, *"Other People's Money," The New Republic*, XCI (August 4, 1937), p. 362. Reprinted by permission of *The New Republic*.

science in a thousand ways—power, machines, all the many features of the motorcar itself, invented by a hundred different men. Among all these things the industry needs a manager. But apparently the manager must be able to take off for his share countless millions as well as the right to shape the social views of his employees and his communities.

But among the ingredients of the Ford myth is this legend—that he is a gentle lover of humanity and that he is the very soul of law and order and civilization in its finest flower. The events of the last few months demonstrate over again a theory I have always entertained: that there is in society no section so given to violence as the conservative, property-loving section. Have you not heard some gentle wisp of an old lady, a model of piety and patriotism, explode into what she would do to the John L. Lewises and similar enemies of society if she had her way?

This is what you have been observing in Dearborn at the plant of this model of evangelical piety and early American love for order. The story of the attack upon the workers at the Ford plant is almost beyond belief. Unfortunately the story, to be understood by the average reader, must be pieced together from the daily accounts over several weeks in newspapers of the NLRB* hearings. I rely upon *The New York Times* for the story.

Walter Reuther, Ford die maker, president of the union's West Side local, and Richard T. Frankensteen, in charge of the union drive among Ford employees, appeared on the Ford overpass to distribute handbills. At the entrance to the plant were about 150 men apparently loitering. A group of these loiterers surrounded the two union men and told them to get the hell off the overpass as it was private property. But before they could do this, Reuther was slugged from behind, thrown to the ground and, while one man gave the orders, others beat and kicked him and then threw him down the iron steps.

Who were these loiterers? Reporters for the Detroit newspapers identified some of them. Arnold Freeman, staff photographer for *The Detroit Times*, visited the River Rouge plant two days before the riot. He recognized men known in Detroit as "dago hoodlums"—a police-court term. One he knew to be a gentleman who had been involved in a recent hold-up case. Freeman asked him if he was up to his old tricks as a muscle man. He answered that he had been hired to take care of these pamphlet-distributing union men. Freeman asked him if he had the downriver gang with him and he said "yes" and pointed out the chief. Freeman recognized him—Angelo Caruso, for whom a felony warrant is extant. One woman testified that when she attempted to distribute leaflets one of the Ford gangsters grabbed her arms, twisted them and wrenched the leaflets from her hands. Let us trust that our good American, Mr. Ford, was duly

* [National Labor Relations Board—ed.]

horrified at the Japanese sentries who are supposed to have shoved and kicked the American girls in Peiping last week.

Ford employees testified:

That plants swarmed with "service" men, some of them plainly armed;

That there was a rule against talking to fellow workers in the plant so drastic that one workman who merely chatted with a companion nearby was dismissed promptly by service men, but was saved by his foreman;

That men who joined the union were promptly dismissed; that foremen at the Ford plant supervised distribution of applications blanks for the Ford Brotherhood of America and ordered employees to sign "if you know what is good for you."

That employees were encouraged to set upon and drive out of the plant men who were known to be engaged in union activities;

That after the riot Harry H. Bennett, personnel director of the Ford Company, was heard to compliment service men on their good work.

This is the same Henry Ford who only fifteen years ago was financing and pushing a drive against the Jews. Now his drive is against the rights of workers to organize. And all the time he poses as the soul of true Americanism. Workers of America should remember that Henry Ford makes automobiles and that he needs customers for them.

I do not mind saying this: that I have rendered at least one small verdict on this man for myself. I own a Ford car. I can tell the world that I will never own another.

EMBATTLED AUTOCRAT [4]

These passages from Keith Sward's biography of Henry Ford could appropriately be put into the next section, because this is a well-documented historical work. They are included here because most of the material was collected during Ford's lifetime. Dr. Sward, in effect, picks up where Leonard left off and exemplifies how Ford's critics saw him in later years.

When the Anti-Semitism of the *Dearborn Independent* was finally challenged in a court of law, Ford beat a hasty retreat. By resorting to one expedient, he escaped the ordeal of having to defend his racial views on the witness stand. A somersault in another direction enabled him to pose as having been utterly innocent of the anti-Jewish activity that had prospered in his name and with his financial support for nearly ten years.

[4] From Keith Sward, *The Legend of Henry Ford* (New York: Holt, Rinehart and Winston, Inc., 1948), pp. 151–53, 278–79, 309–13, 368–69. Copyright © 1948 by Keith Sward. Reprinted by permission of Holt, Rinehart and Winston, Russell & Volkening, Inc., and the author.

This double act of face-saving was performed by Cameron, the editor of the *Dearborn Independent*, and by Harry Bennett, then Ford's chief private detective.

Both of these measures of defense were aimed at Aaron Sapiro, a Jewish lawyer and promoter. Sapiro had come into some prestige and a small fortune by organizing marketing associations among the farmers of the country. When the *Dearborn Independent* accused him of fleecing his clients, he filed a million-dollar damage suit against Ford. The case came to trial in Detroit in March 1927.

Ford was represented in the action by an imposing staff of seven attorneys. All but one of this galaxy of able counsel were members of the Detroit bar. The single outsider, engaged for psychological effect, was Senator James A. Reed of Missouri. Ford's advisers fully expected to find the plaintiff represented by a "Jew lawyer from New York." Much to their surprise, however, Sapiro walked into court with William Henry Gallagher, a prominent Detroit attorney who was an Irish Catholic.

At the trial, W. J. Cameron, the author of "Mr. Ford's Own Page" and the star witness for the defense, simply offered himself up as a sacrifice on the altar of public opinion. On the stand for five days and subjected to a merciless cross-examination, Cameron assumed full responsibility for every word the *Dearborn Independent* had ever printed. He strove, under fire, to absolve Ford of any complicity whatever in the attack on Sapiro or any other Jew by asserting that he alone, as editor of the *Dearborn Independent*, had the power to frame the paper's editorial policy.[5]

Under oath, Cameron contended that Ford had never read the *Dearborn Independent* in his presence. His own judgment in the management of the paper, he testified, had been final and absolute in all matters. No advance copy, he swore, had ever required Ford's personal approval. Cameron then professed that he had never discussed with Ford "any article" on "any Jew." He stated, finally, that he had never so much as talked with Ford about the stand taken by the *Dearborn Independent* on any public question.

Some of this testimony was the whole truth; the rest, half-truth or fabrication. In the first place it had never been necessary for Ford to keep close watch over his newspaper. Ernest Liebold had done that for him. It was Liebold rather than Ford who had dictated the paper's editorial policy and censored its content again and again. In so doing, Liebold had always moved with authority: he was Ford's personal secretary as well as general manager of the parent corporation, the Dearborn Publishing Co., under whose auspices the *Dearborn Independent* was issued. More than that, Cameron had never required close editorial supervision. By the time he

---

[5] *Detroit News*, March 21, 1927; March 12, 1927; March 25, 1927; *The New York Times*, March 25, 1927.

took the stand in the Sapiro case, he had been fraternizing with Ford and Liebold off and on for seven years. He knew the foibles of both men by heart.

Nor was Cameron's declaration that he had never discussed "any article" on "any Jew" in Ford's presence the same as saying that he had never talked with Ford on the subject of Jews in general. In a narrow sense, this protestation may have been true. The facts belie any broader construction. Pipp* has told how Cameron had to be prodded into writing any anti-Semitic pieces at all. Liebold, his immediate superior, would hardly have purchased the "Protocols" and placed this document on Cameron's desk without having had Ford's tacit consent. Moreover, years before Sapiro filed suit, Ford and Cameron together once spent an entire afternoon vainly trying to infect Dean Marquis with their racial virus. Several months after the termination of the Sapiro case, Cameron impeached his own court testimony by refusing at first to credit the news that Ford had authorized a public retraction of his alleged anti-Semitism.[6]

*   *   *

It was Ford's voicing of the doctrine of high wages and low prices, however, that finally crowned him as the greatest of the mass producers. Here, it seemed, was a builder of the modern world who practiced what he preached as he spread the creed that no mechanized civilization could survive unless it could absorb what it produced. The apostle of the New Messiah seemed to have hit on the answer to war, to the riddle of the business cycle, to the plague of overproduction and the maldistribution of wealth. It was this claim to economic statesmanship that led Edward A. Filene, the Boston philanthropist, to nominate Ford in 1930 as a logical candidate for the Nobel Peace Prize. But years before Filene made this suggestion, the man on the street had come to revere Ford for the same reasons. To Ford's person the plain people of the world had long since projected the American dream of plenty. In him the masses had identified the benevolent hero of the capitalist saga, the capitalist who had the wit to make capitalism work.

In his rise to national sainthood, Ford won the hearts of men for the further reason that his career seemed to resolve the dominant moral conflicts of the age. This American millionaire, living under a code of Protestant capitalism in a society which venerates goodness and rewards success, appeared to be two-in-one. He was the empire builder who shared with others as he gathered in the sheaves for himself. He was reputed rich and good, shrewd and fair, acquisitive and generous, powerful and kindly,

* [Edwin G. Pipp, a Detroit newspaperman, was the first editor of the *Dearborn Independent*—ed.]
[6] New York *World*, July 8, 1927.

self-seeking and benevolent. This demigod of the machine age had some-how stitched together the incompatibles of the struggle for existence. He was the idol of an American middle class which wants to eat its cake and have it too, the venerated symbol of a system under which people aspire to be neither so self-seeking that they lose caste nor so good that they must spend their days in poverty.

Once in motion, the process of beatification which set Ford apart from other men kept growing of its own accord. It began feeding on itself. Adulation of the man became infectious and cumulative. His fame waxed to heroic proportions under its own momentum. Labor leaders, university presidents and foreign dignitaries applauded him. He was decorated by three European governments. Among the ranks conferred upon him by more than one institution of higher learning were the titles of honorary Doctor of Engineering and honorary Doctor of Law. His recognition trav-eled far beyond the field of his achievement. One hall of fame after an-other opened its portals to this revered figure. In 1926, said one South American author, Ford ranked in public esteem in Brazil on a parity with Cromwell, Bacon, Columbus, Pasteur, and Moses. A group of American college students once ranked the manufacturer as the third greatest figure of all time, surpassed in their judgment only by Napoleon Bonaparte and Jesus Christ. For years the newspapers of Detroit made a habit of referring to Ford as "the sage of Dearborn."

* * *

Once its tentacles were fully grown, the Ford Service Department bred a state of mind in and about Detroit that could be duplicated only in those localities which have written the darker pages of American indus-trial history. In Ford's case, however, an oppressive discipline manifested itself, not in a provincial steel town nor in a backwoods mining com-munity, but in one of the country's largest metropolitan centers. The strained air that became characteristic of the Ford organization was per-haps unique in exempting from its spells no one in the corporation, high or low.

The temper of the Rouge was exemplified, as of 1939, even by the air of the reception room in the company's Engineering Laboratory. The room itself—a small, cheerless cell in an otherwise spacious building—was an architectural reminder that on Ford property even the ease and com-fort of the business caller were out of place. In Ford's waiting room, unlike the Packard lobby or the General Motors corridor, were no comfortable lounges or brass cuspidors arranged for the convenience of the guest. While waiting for an interview, the Ford visitor who wished to smoke had to step outside. If he was familiar with the traditions of the Rouge, he took the further precaution of driving to his conference only in a Ford car.

Admitted to the suite of a Ford executive, or to the publicity office of the corporation, the casual visitor was likewise struck by the tense, guarded manner of the employees. This uneasy demeanor seemed to be, first, a by-product of the cult of man-worship that had long prevailed at Ford's. It also savored of the chilling effect of Ford Service. These executive mannerisms at Dearborn had several variants. The Ford publicist who gave one an audience in 1939 was ready, as ever, to eulogize The Man. The Man's name, when it entered the conversation, was always, reverently, "Mr. Henry" Ford. The Ford spokesman appeared to his caller as though he were walking on eggs for fear some Tom, Dick or Harry—other than Ford or Bennett—might be taken for an entity in his own right. If any Ford subordinate was inadvertently singled out because of some noteworthy performance, the Ford publicist would, as often as not, instantly qualify that distinction with some such remark as "Oh, just forget I mentioned that. So-and-so is just one of Mr. Henry Ford's men. He wouldn't want his name known. He wouldn't want to stick his neck out."

A General Motors man, on the other hand, was by common agreement at this period much less inhibited. In his shop talk with an outsider he was far less self-conscious and much less idolatrous. He would speak of *his* work or of the *corporation*. He could hold forth more freely on ideas or on the trends of the trade. Names, big or little, might come and go in his conversation. If he mentioned the "boss" at all, it was "Sloan" or, before the Second World War, "Bill Knudsen."

The public relations man at the Ford Motor Co. during the Bennett regime ran to type in still another sense. He seemed to be parroting phrases committed to memory; he talked at his listener rather than to him. He would say repetitiously, "Everyone knows that Mr. Bennett is a man of unusual physical courage," or "Well, of course, Mr. Ford has a twenty-track mind." Officials who filled similar positions elsewhere in the trade, on the other hand, seemed less forced, much readier to talk. Within limits they spilled out at will whatever thoughts came to mind. Moreover, by contrast with their peers at the Ford Motor Co., the head men at Chrysler's or General Motors were not only easier to talk to, but a hundred times easier to see in the first place.

Even among their familiars, Ford's administrators, hedged about by Ford and Bennett, acquired a reputation for this same nervous pulling-in. Under the Bennett regime there was little of the interoffice banter that the most casual observer could overhear in the General Motors building on Grand Boulevard, and almost none of the executive manner that looks like soldiering but is actually a method of doing business.

The Ford dealer was likewise more constrained than most of his competitors. He did not feel at liberty to unburden himself on company policy, other than in the presence of his closest friends. One of the firm's energetic Eastern dealers entered into such a discussion with a stranger whom he had met through a mutual acquaintance in 1939 by remarking, with evident embarrassment, "I'd be perfectly willing to go into this subject with you, if I could be absolutely sure who you are. Harry Bennett has some pretty slick customers at work around the country. As it is, I've stuck my neck out pretty far already."

Employees on every rung of the Ford ladder came to respond to the eccentric, tight discipline and the catlike watchfulness of Ford Service by showing every manner of job anxiety. This state of mind at Ford's was a common subject of gossip in the trade. *Fortune* magazine in its issue of December 1933, could observe that "Mr. Ford's organization does show extreme evidence of being ruled primarily by fear of the job." As a rule, Ford's managers, having more to lose, came to watch their jobs more nervously than the man at the Rouge who swept the floor.

On the lower tiers of the Ford organization, Ford Service gave rise to any number of unmistakable industrial neuroses. These "shop complaints" went all the way from mild states of anxiety to advanced nervous symptoms that were fit material for a psychopathic ward. Thus conditioned, the personality of any Ford employee was subjected to a process of subtle and profound degradation.

Any number of idiosyncrasies bore witness to the stiffening effect of regimentation within the Rouge. Chatting or fraternizing with workmates during the lunch hour was taboo in the old days which lasted twenty years or more. It was then the rule during the noonday spell to see a Ford employee squat on the floor, glum and uncommunicative, munching his food in almost complete isolation. The locked-in manner of the Ford worker supposedly at ease was remarked by Raymond J. Daniell who observed in *The New York Times* on October 31, 1937, "The visitor (at the Rouge) is struck by the restraint among the workers; even in moments of idleness, men stand apart from one another."

Ford men, before long, became noted for their ingenuity in circumventing the ironclad law against talking at their work. They developed an art of covert speech known as the "Ford whisper." Masters of this language, like inmates in a penal institution, could communicate in undertones without taking their eyes from their work. If Ford or Sorensen were about to tour the plant, even the plant foremen knew how to spread the word by resorting to the "grapevine."

Ford's tool and die men used to be governed by the same taboo, though their work by its very nature compelled them to move about. Long ago, these craftsmen invented their own brand of hidden talk. Their technique was to exchange small talk while gesticulating in mock earnestness at parts of a lathe, or while feigning interest in a blueprint. One highly intelligent artisan in this department invented a type of "Ford speech" all his own. He learned to talk like a ventriloquist. After spending ten years in Ford's service, this man became the laughing stock of his wife and friends, for the habit of talking out of the side of his mouth without moving his lips finally became ungovernable; he began to talk that way uncon-sciously, at home or in the most casual conversation with someone outside after working hours.

"Fordization of the face" was once the rule among all Ford men at work, inasmuch as humming, whistling or even smiling on the job were, in the judgment of Ford Service, evidence of soldiering or insubordination. John Gallo, a Rouge employee, was discharged in November 1940— caught in the act of "smiling," after having committed an earlier breach of "laughing with the other fellows," and slowing down the line "maybe half a minute." At a formal hearing on the case, a state labor referee gave it as his opinion that while a shop rule prohibiting the least show of levity may have been acceptable under the "Puritans" and in the day of the old "overseer," such a ban was hardly in keeping with the standards of "this enlightened age." Inasmuch as he could establish no demonstrable con-nection between "smiling" and efficiency in this case the referee ruled that Gallo was entitled to full benefits under the unemployment com-pensation act.

*   *   *

When all the leading manufacturers of the trade came to terms with the union several years ahead of Ford, there was a period when labor's status at the Ford Motor Co. was, on every score, the most backward in the industry. During that interval, the men at the Rouge could enumerate airtight grievances that held for their shop alone. Their wages trailed the field. Their speed-up had no parallel. Their jobs were the least stable in the business. If maimed at their benches, they were less assured of ade-quate protection than any other group of automobile workers in the state of Michigan. Nor was there at this time or earlier any plant in the com-munity so spy-ridden as the Rouge or so drenched with a psychology that was calculated to break the spirit of men.

Ford more than once discussed men in general in terms that were quite in keeping with the facts of his labor history. On such occasions he gave it as his frank opinion that the man who works with his hands is a nobody. Most of the jobs in his mill, he asserted in one of his books, have no appeal for "men with brains." [7] According to his autobiography, the "majority of minds" are blessed by nature with a capacity to take the "drudgery" of mass production and like it.[8] Again, in his judgment, the man on the

---

[7] Henry Ford, *Today and Tomorrow*, pp. 160, 183.
[8] Henry Ford, *My Life and Work*, p. 103.

street is a congenital nitwit, doomed to failure. "It is evident," he wrote in the story of his life, "that a majority of the people in the world are not mentally—even if they are physically—capable of making a good living." [9]

Inasmuch as this contempt for the common man was made so evident by job conditions at the Rouge, feelings of unrest finally engulfed the Ford personnel. For a decade or more these feelings lay dormant and smoldering. Their existence was detected by the acute observer, however, years before they burst into the open.

As far back as 1927, B. C. Forbes, the financial analyst, expressed the conviction that if every employer in America were to take after Ford in his treatment of men, ". . . this country would be headed for the gravest trouble." [10] In arriving at this judgment, Forbes said he had received more unsolicited letters of complaint from Ford workers than from any other body of employes in the nation.[11] A year later, in 1928, in the course of gauging the morale of the Ford personnel, a reporter of *The New York Times* called Ford "an industrial fascist—the Mussolini of Detroit." This journalist cited Ford's organization as the world's outstanding example of complete autocratic control of a vast industry.[12]

[9] *Ibid.*, p. 77.
[10] *Forbes*, May 15, 1927.
[11] *Ibid.*, May 1, 1927.
[12] *The New York Times*, January 8, 1928.

PART THREE

FORD IN HISTORY

Henry Ford is a recent enough figure so that there is a problem of separating historical judgment from contemporary opinion. The task of evaluation has been greatly assisted by the action of his heirs and successors in establishing the Ford Archives in Dearborn and making the records available to scholars, and also in sponsoring a monumental study of Henry Ford and the Ford Motor Company by a group of historians headed by Allan Nevins.

The selections included here look back at Henry Ford from various perspectives. Charles E. Sorensen speaks from his long career as a Ford executive— far longer than any other of Ford's lieutenants. He began as a patternmaker in 1905 and rose to be head of production. When he left in 1944, the scapegoat for the disappointing progress of the Willow Run aircraft factory, he was thoroughly familiar with the inside workings of the Ford Motor Company and the personality of its founder. Peter F. Drucker appraises the significance of the Ford accomplishment from the point of view of a profound student of corporate organization and its impact on the structure of society. William Greenleaf, a former member of Nevins' staff, is the leading authority on the Selden patent case and Ford's ideas on the patent system.

There are evaluations of Ford, generally sympathetic, by Roger Burlingame, outstanding American historian of technology, and from the third and concluding volume of the Nevins study. The eminent economist John Kenneth Galbraith presents a dissenting opinion. Father R. L. Bruckberger, a perceptive French student of the American scene, offers an original interpretation of Ford's place in history. Roger Butterfield has a reappraisal of the "History is bunk" legend and Ford's attitude toward history. Finally, in place of an epilogue I have included excerpts from my book The American Automobile.

11

Charles E. Sorensen:
"No Mystic or Genius"[1]

Henry Ford was no mystic or genius. He was a responsible person with determination to do his work as he believed it should be done. This sense of responsibility was one of his strongest traits.

I often tried to persuade Mr. Ford to diversify his business; get into the food-producing field, because he liked farming, or take up something like Sears, Roebuck or Marshall Field. He would have nothing to do with the idea. "I don't want any more business," he said.

I also tried to get him to expand the auto field. I felt we could build a near monopoly. "Let us shoot at seventy-five per cent of market requirements," I urged.

"I don't want any more than thirty per cent," he replied.

How right he was! If Ford Motor Company had seventy-five per cent of the auto business today, it would be prosecuted as a monopoly. He actually welcomed the competition that was looming before us, though in later years he had suspicion amounting to hallucination that bankers and General Motors were out to ruin him.

The ability to sense signs of the times and to counteract forces that showed danger signals was almost uncanny. I would go to him with problems that looked insurmountable. Nothing appeared to frighten him. In the early days of the New Deal he was threatened with all sorts of government reprisal for defying the National Industrial Recovery Act, that the government would take over his company if he didn't sign up and display the Blue Eagle. He replied, "Go ahead. The government will then be in the automobile business. Let's see if they can manage it better than I can."

That stopped General "Iron Pants" Johnson [General Hugh Johnson, NRA administrator] and President Roosevelt.

There is no doubt that Henry Ford had courage. Probably he will never be glorified for his peace ship excursion; but no one can tell me it didn't take courage to undertake it. It took courage, too, to fight the Selden

[1] From Charles E. Sorensen, with Samuel T. Williamson, *My Forty Years with Ford* (New York: W. W. Norton & Company, Inc., 1956), pp. 24–25, 26–28, 128–29. Copyright © 1956 by Charles E. Sorensen. Reprinted by permission of A. Watkins, Inc.

patent, to hold to his fixed idea of a cheap car, to battle dividend-hungry boards of directors, to build River Rouge plant in the face of stockholder opposition.

*   *   *

New things stimulated him. If a suggestion appealed to him, he first showed it in a quick flash of his eyes and an approving smile. I saw the same characteristic reaction in Henry Ford II. As soon as Mr. Ford saw an idea developed and at work, it was out of date. He never ran out of ideas. In his prime he was loaded with them, and it was impossible to keep up with him unless one had vision and initiative enough to anticipate them and stay ahead of him. Like all men in his position, he was pestered by inventors and cranks, all with ideas they wanted him to look at. His answer to most of them was, "I can't do it. I have so many ideas of my own that I can't keep up with them; so how can I devote time to yours?"

Constant ferment—keep things stirred up and other people guessing— was the elder Ford's working formula for progress. Initially, that lay behind his putting Harry Bennett on Edsel's neck, but what began with occasional harassment became a habit with Bennett, who in so doing drove a wider wedge between father and son. Henry Ford's greatest failure was in expecting Edsel to be like him. Edsel's greatest victory, despite all obstacles, was in being *himself*. I saw all this, but it is a story I must relate later because it needs greater detail and the background of events.

He was so much of an individualist that no one ever really knew him. The most frequent question I've been asked about Henry Ford is "Was he modest?" According to Webster, modesty means decent reserve and propriety, a humble estimate of oneself in comparison with others, shyness and a sensitive shrinking from anything indelicate.

No, Henry Ford was not modest. He did a lot for people he liked, but he didn't want his staff to be in the public eye. No one else in the organization could stand out and above him. He pretended to be humble when with people who did not know him. But I knew this was an act. He never could be humble when around us. When I saw both sides of him, I knew that he lacked modesty.

He sought publicity. There was nothing shy about him in that. Shyness is a tendency to shrink from observation. He wanted to be observed. Henry Ford and Arthur Brisbane of the Hearst newspapers were friendly. Brisbane had a farm and was greatly interested in the tractors we were making. He wrote up our plant and experimental farm at Dearborn but neglected to play up Henry Ford, and he learned from the Detroit office of the Hearst papers that he had offended him. I told him that Henry Ford did not want his staff to receive publicity. It was dangerous for anyone to get newspaper notice. I was not exaggerating. After the name of Henry Ford became a household word, men in Ford Motor Company who might temporarily get more publicity than he did aroused his jealousy. One by one they were purged, a process familiar in personal dictatorships.

*   *   *

Henry Ford had no ideas on mass production. He wanted to build a lot of autos. He was determined but, like everyone else at that time, he didn't know how. In later years he was glorified as the originator of the mass production idea. Far from it; he just grew into it, like the rest of us. The essential tools and the final assembly line with its many integrated feeders resulted from an organization which was continually experimenting and improvising to get better production.

It became apparent that we should revamp the plant to cut down operation time in the different parts assemblies and speed up deliveries to the big ground-floor room where the cars were put together. It was for this purpose that I installed the first conveyer system.

Radiators were put together on the second floor. Originally tubes and fins came from a supplier, and our people inserted tubes one at a time into the fins. This required the expense and handling effort of keeping a considerable stock on hand. Then we stamped out fins on our own press, conveyed these and other parts on belts past various assembly operations, and sent the finished radiators by conveyer downstairs to car assembly. Things went along nicely until one of those rare occasions when Mr. Couzens went into the plant. On that morning he came inside the manufacturing building and asked George, the doorman, where Mr. Ford was. At the same time he noticed the radiators dangling overhead on their way to the assembly line. Looking up and down, he apparently wasn't too pleased with what he saw. "What's all this? " he asked.

"That is one of Mr. Sorensen's accomplishments," George said.

Later Mr. Ford warned me: "Look out for Couzens. He is on the warpath over the radiator conveyer. When he calls for you, better be prepared, but don't take him too seriously."

I didn't have to wait long for that call. Mr. Couzens went at me hammer and tongs. How could anybody spend money like that without his knowing anything about it? I told him that I had never had a chance to explain what a great saving it was. I described the situation in the past, how great stacks of material piled up in the radiator department awaiting assembly, how all radiators were taken by truck down to the first floor where another large stock accumulated ready to be carried to be bolted to the cars. I gave him cost figures and the hours of labor involved in this cumbersome procedure.

Couzens listened with great interest, then asked what the conveyer had cost. Given that, he figured that the savings in just a few days' operations paid for the conveyer. This experience was similar to many that I had with Mr. Couzens; when convinced that initial expenditures meant long-range economy and more production, he made no trouble. He never found fault after that with similar developments in other parts assemblies, and it wasn't long before I got a nice increase in salary.

This proved beyond question and further opposition the success of the conveyer system. Years later, in *My Life and Work*, a book which was written for him, Mr. Ford said that the conveyer-assembly idea occurred to him after watching the reverse process in packing houses, where hogs and steers were triced up by hind legs on an overhead conveyer and disassembled. This is a rationalization long after the event. Mr. Ford had nothing to do with originating, planning, and carrying out the assembly line. He encouraged the work, his vision to try unorthodox methods was an example to us; and in that there is glory enough for all.

12

Peter F. Drucker: "A Principle of Social Order"[1]

In 1928, at the peak of the boom following World War I, Henry Ford officially proclaimed the New Millenium of mass production; his article bore the significant title: "Machinery, the New Messiah." Technology was also seen as the decisive element in "Fordism" by Lenin—one of Ford's greatest admirers in the early twenties. His slogan, that Communism is "Socialism plus Electrification," indicates a completely technological view of the new principle he was so eager to adopt.

The easy optimism of these pioneering days has long since evaporated; the collapse of 1929 marked its end. But the opponents and critics of mass production who have held the center of the stage since, also see the essence of mass production in a mechanical principle. Technology is the villain in Aldous Huxley's *Brave New World*, which, published at the bottom of the Depression, expressed the disappointment of the earlier hopes. It was the villain in Karel Capek's R. U. R., which gave us the word "robot." It was the enemy in Charlie Chaplin's "Our Times." However much the Henry Ford of "Machinery, the New Messiah" and the Charlie Chaplin of "Our Times" may differ as to the effect of the new development on man and his society, they agree on its nature. The revolutionary principle is a new technique, a new machine or a new way to utilize machines, a new arrangement of physical inanimate forces. The very slogan of most of our discussions is the "subordination of man to the machine."

But if we actually analyze this new so-called technology, we shall find that it is not a "technology" at all. It is not an arrangement of physical forces. It is a principle of social order. This was true of Ford's work. He made not one mechanical invention or discovery; everything mechanical he used was old and well known. Only his concept of human organization for work was new.

The mass-production revolution is the culmination of a major change

[1] From Peter F. Drucker, *The New Society* (New York: Harper & Row, Publishers, 1950), pp. 19–20, 22–25. Copyright © 1949, 1950 by Peter F. Drucker. Reprinted by permission of Harper & Row, Publishers, and William Heinemann Ltd.

in the social order that has been going on since the Industrial Revolution began two hundred years ago. In the mass-production revolution the basic principles of industrialism have come to full maturity. And through the mass-producticn revolution they have become universal—world-wide as well as all-embracing. What started out as a technology two hundred years ago, has in the mass-production revolution grown into a society. In the mass-production principle we have not only a solvent of the traditional social order of pre-industrial society. We have a new principle of social organization.

*   *   *

Because nobody in the social order of modern industry makes a product, "integration" also assumes a new meaning. A product can only be made if the operations and motions of a great many individuals are put together and integrated into a pattern. It is this pattern that is actually productive, not the individual. Modern industry requires a group organization far exceeding in forethought, precision and cohesion, anything we have ever witnessed.

It was Henry Ford who provided the original example of integration on which all later industry has modeled itself. The coordination of the labor of men with the flow of materials which he developed in the twenties at the new River Rouge plant synchronized and integrated not only the work of the 80,000 men working there and the materials and parts with which they worked. It attempted to carry the same integration of work, rhythm and timing all the way back to the stage of raw-material production and procurement—the digging of iron ore in Northern Michigan, or the tapping of rubber trees in Brazil—and forward into the sales of new cars by the dealers. This plan would have embraced the work of millions of men within a time span of two or three years. Ford's attempt itself failed—being both too ambitious and premature. But the Russian Five-Year Plans are essentially modeled after Ford's concept. And in the great landings on the European Continent during World War II, Ford's concepts were applied to masses of men much larger and to operations much more complex than he had ever tried to deal with.

Mass production is actually a considerably more skilled system of production than any previous one. Much more new skill is required for integration than has been eliminated by specialization. However, the new skill is not manual, it is not knowledge of tools or of materials. It is partly technical and theoretical: knowledge of principles and processes. Partly it is social: skill in the organization of men for work in a close group and in fitting together their operations, their speeds and their abilities. Above all, the new "skill" required is the ability to see, to understand

and even to produce a pattern; and that is by definition imaginative ability of a high, almost of an artistic, order.

One example which shows this clearly is the story of the difficulties encountered during the last war with the production of a carrier-based plane for the Navy. When Pearl Harbor came, this plane was the only tested model suitable for warfare in the Pacific; yet only a dozen or so had actually been made—and by a small firm of airplane designers. At once the Navy needed not dozens but thousands of these planes. The original designers were quite incapable of producing such quantities; they did not even have the blueprints needed for mass production, as they had built each plane by hand in their small workshop. One of the large companies took over, converted hastily some of its best plants, put its best engineers, mechanics and skilled workers to work and began producing the plane. Yet not one plane could actually be turned out until the theoretical work—the analysis of the plane; its breakdown into the component parts; the breakdown of each part into subassemblies; the breakdown of the subassemblies into individual operations and motions; and the reintegration of operations into subassemblies, of subassemblies into parts, of parts into the plane—had been completed. It was work done entirely on paper—with some hundred tons of blueprints as the yield. It was done entirely on the basis of general principles. Airplane experts proved of no value whatsoever. The actual job had to be done by men who had never worked on plane production before. It was a slow job, taking almost a year during which nothing was produced. But once it had been done, the plant went almost immediately into full production; five weeks after the last blueprint had been completed, the plant turned out planes at the rate of 6,000 a year.

Without the integration there would not only be no product, there would be no work for anybody. For the individual as well as for society, the really productive element in modern industrial society is a concept— one is tempted to say a vision: the view of the whole, the vision of a pattern. In this pattern no one man is by himself productive. But the pattern would become disorder, the entire organization would cease to make sense, production would stop altogether, were the least operation left undone. There is no one "decisive" operation, but also no single "unnecessary" one.

In its interplay between "specialization" and "integration"—between the fundamentally unessential and replaceable, and the fundamentally essential and irreplaceable, character of each and every operation—the social order of the mass-production technology reveals itself as basically a hierarchial order. But it is a very peculiar kind.

It is not altogether unique. The little we know about the men who built the great medieval cathedrals indicates that they worked in a pattern of specialization and integration strikingly similar to the modern mass-production factory. Another analogy would be a ritual dance put on by a tribe, or a theatrical performance: certainly a troup of actors producing a play work together on pretty much the same basis. Closer still would be the analogy to a symphony orchestra.

These parallels serve, however, only to point up the novel features of the mass-production order. The dancer in a tribal group may have only one small part. He may know that he can never get a big part if, for instance, the big parts are reserved for the chiefs. But if his operation is sufficiently similar to that of the leading man, he can understand the work of the star and also see the whole and his relation to it. The tympani player in the orchestra will never play the first violin, let alone conduct. But he can read the score—indeed, he has to know it fairly well to be able to come in at the right moment. The same relationship existed between apprentice or unskilled helper in a cathedral "production line" and the great craftsman and artist on the one hand, and the cathedral itself on the other.

In the social pattern of mass production, however, the difference between operation and operation, between job and job is so profound, the specialization carried so far, that the worker can have no immediate understanding, usually not even a superficial knowledge, of the next job. The relationship to the product is even less clear. The whole and the relationship of the individuals to it is visible only to the few people at the top—the conductors, to use the analogy of the orchestra. They see the pattern, understand the order, experience the vision. But the great many below do not unaided see anything but chaos, disorder and nonsense; and the further they are away from the top, the less able are they to see sense, order and purpose.

13
William Greenleaf: Ford and the Patent System[1]

Incontestably, the several approaches Ford made to the A. L. A. M. were motivated by self-interest. He was struggling for survival and recognition. The Selden association threatened to close the door against his entry into the industry and to cut off his vision of a mass-produced automobile. The Selden patent was a barrier to his future, and he saw that it must be battered down. It was incomprehensible that a fiction of the patent laws should thwart his own self-realization. "There's too much tradition in all human activity, too much respect for mere precedent," said Ford many years later. "If it stands in the way of progress it must be broken down." [2] Even at this time, long before he was acclaimed as a prophet of the machine age, Ford regarded himself as an agent of social progress.

It may be argued that his change of attitude toward the A. L. A. M. was the maneuver of an opportunist. But this does not lessen the truth that expedient conduct may undergo a sea-change and become principled courage when the defense of personal interest takes on the larger dimensions of moral conviction. "What is the greatest thing in the world—your greatest ambition? " Ford was once asked. "To be free—a free man," he shot back.[3] After his final conference with Frederic L. Smith, * Ford knew that he could not be free so long as the Selden patent clouded the destiny he had marked out for himself.

The reasons for his opposition were largely personal. His rebuff by the A. L. A. M. disparaged his ability as a designer and builder of automobiles. Ford's reaction was shaped by his instinct of craftsmanship and the stock of ideas he had absorbed during his youth on a Michigan farm. It was also influenced by his emerging views on the patent system and,

---

[1] From William Greenleaf, *Monopoly on Wheels* (Detroit: Wayne State University Press, 1961), pp. 112–14, 187–88, 247–50. Copyright © 1961 by Wayne State University Press. Reprinted by permission of Wayne State University Press.

[2] Waldemar Kaempffert, "The Mussolini of Highland Park," *The New York Times*, January 8, 1928.

[3] "Henry Ford at Bay," *Forum*, LXII (August, 1919), 241.

* [President of the Olds Motor Works and a leading figure in the A. L. A. M.—ed.]

finally, by the native shrewdness that characterized his decisions as an industrialist. Ford's shift from the role of suppliant to rebel cannot be understood unless the springs of his motivation are explored.

By the time the Seldon challenge arose, Ford had devoted about a decade of thought and labor to planning and building motor cars. He jealously prized as a hard-won creation the automobile which bore his name. That car, like those of other automobile pioneers, owed nothing to the teachings of the Selden patent. As Ford pointed out, he "knew it was the product of his own brain and no man on earth was entitled to any 'rake-off' from that particular car." [4] His pride as a craftsman was piqued by an attempt to exclude him from the industry on the pretext that he had trespassed on Selden's primacy. "Selden Pat *Not Workable*," Ford scrawled in one of the vest-pocket notebooks he kept for jotting down his thoughts. This brief verdict was his final repudiation, as a craftsman and engineer, of the Selden patent. [5]

Another compelling reason for his decision to make war upon the patent was his deep-seated distrust of monopoly. Ford drew many of his ideas and notions from a Midwestern rural culture that had a strong flavor of Populist discontent. With many Midwesterners of his generation he shared a hatred of industrial combinations and Eastern financial power. As William J. Cameron remarked, Ford was "raised on that terrible fear of monopolistic power holding everything down." [6] In his young manhood, Ford may have responded sympathetically to the attacks which Midwestern Populists, moved by a bitter animus against patent monopolies, launched against the Bell System and other large aggregations. More immediately, his opposition to monopoly was reinforced by the knowledge that one or more of the licensed Detroit auto manufacturers were intent upon driving him out of business.

As for the patent system, Ford regarded it as at best a necessary evil. He had a reasoned view of invention as "a matter of evolution." The Selden patent bore the inescapable marks of evolution, but Selden claimed nothing less than the credit for genesis. Ford was fond of saying there was "very little new under the sun." "I have taken out 300 or 400 patents in all countries," he said in 1921, "and I undertake to say there is not a new thing in our car." Believing that very few inventions were truly original, Ford held that no one had a right to take out a patent and prevent others from using it. "Patent monopoly awakens his fierce re-

---

[4] "Why Henry Ford Fought the Selden Patents," New York *Herald*, January 14, 1906.

[5] Henry Ford Diaries and Notes, Fair Lane Papers, Accession 1, Box 13, Ford Archives (italics in the original); see also, "Henry Ford Explains Why He Gives Away $10,000,000," *The New York Times*, January 11, 1914.

[6] Reminiscences of W. J. Cameron, Oral History Section, Ford Archives.

sentment," said a journalist in 1918, when Ford was a candidate for the United States Senate. At that time Ford declared: "If I should go to the Senate, one of the first things I would do would be to begin an agitation for the abolition of all patent laws. They don't . . . stimulate invention—that is an exploded theory. But they do exploit the consumer, and place a heavy burden on productive industry." [7] They were the nemesis of free competition.

Finally, Ford's canny business sense told him that he would gain rather than lose by fighting the Selden patent. For motorists who in 1903 could afford a car that cost upwards of $2,000, the A. L. A. M. royalty of $1\frac{1}{4}$ per cent, which was added to the retail price, was not an onerous levy. It could, however, be a burden for the purchaser of moderate means who was unable to pay more than $1,000 for an automobile. The tax was in conflict with the low-price policy that Ford envisioned. In addition, should Ford attain an annual output running into the thousands, his total royalty payments would represent a sizable sum. This money, he probably calculated, might be used to better effect in defending an infringement suit.

* * *

His involvement in the Selden patent war thrust upon Henry Ford the beginnings of a legend. The years of the litigation saw his rise as the most controversial figure in the formative period of the motor car industry. Well before the suit ended, the automobile world came to know him as its most ardent champion of the principle of free enterprise.

Ford's role in the Selden case drew added meaning from his emergence as the leading manufacturer of a low-cost car produced in quantity for a mass market. This development, wholly unanticipated by the A. L. A. M., did much to detract from the Selden cause. Where the licensed association offered assurances that the patent was valid, and exacted a royalty for which there was no equivalent in the product, Ford stressed the positive contribution of a sturdy car designed for the people. Where the A. L. A. M. sought to exclude venture capital, Ford waged grim resistance against privileged monopoly on the traditional ground of unfettered competitive enterprise. By endowing his own struggle for a place in the sun with a luminous appeal to fundamental principles, he translated a wearisome patent suit into one man's struggle for the right to enjoy unhampered opportunity. This was a potent theme in a day when the politics of Progressivism was sweeping the land and the movement for

[7] Judson C. Welliver, "Henry Ford, Dreamer and Worker," *American Review of Reviews*, LXVI (November, 1921), 493; Willis J. Abbott, "Our Job as a Nation," quoted in *Henry Ford v. the Tribune Co. et al.*, Transcript of Certain Articles, p. 60.

social democracy was still nourished by the hopes and ambitions of the small businessman.

The first half of the Selden suit coincided with a marked change in Ford's personal fortunes. His ascendancy to a dominant position within the company paralleled his growing reputation in the industry. In 1906, he bought out the stock interest of his former partner, Alex Y. Malcomson, and a year later became president and majority stockholder of the company. Although his augmented holdings naturally reinforced his determination that the Selden patent must be broken, Ford's material interest was never paramount to his moral conviction that Selden was a trespasser upon individual creativeness and initiative. After the Ford Motor Company gave proof of its staying power, Ford never feared the patent as a real threat to the prosperity of the venture. The company reinvested its cash earnings, expanded its operations, increased its sales and profits by the year, and declared handsome dividends at frequent intervals. Such unslackened progress would have been impossible had the Selden suit actually hobbled the company. Indeed, even as the case was under way, the Ford Motor Company took the first step toward the epochal achievement of the American automobile industry.

*   *   *

Ford's unorthodox position is attributable to the refusal of the A. L. A. M. to grant him a Selden license in 1903, but during his lifetime it reflected more than a persistent animus against the shade of the long-departed "Selden trust." His involvement in the Selden suit aroused a sharp and rankling distaste for the American patent system that he never overcame. More than that, it implanted a determination to secure the necessary elements of a dynamic technology without laying himself under tribute to others. Yet, as much as Ford detested the patent system, he could not divorce himself from it. In an industrial order where inventions become private property by virtue of the patent grant, the Ford Motor Company has meticulously observed the formal requirements of the patent laws. But Ford himself never gave an inch in his conviction, which developed and hardened during the Selden case, that patents are worthless unless they contribute to the common store of industrial and social wealth. It was thus that the patent policy of the Ford Motor Company, a policy over which Ford exerted direct control during his active career, became the projection of one man's view that the inventive process is ultimately measured and tested by practical consequences.

His experience in the Selden case taught Ford that a patent right used only for collecting royalties is detrimental to the growth of a free and progressive technology. His inflexible attitude was expressed in a statement he made in 1925: "Patents are silly things when they are used to hinder any industry. No man has a right to profit by a patent only. That produces parasites, men who are willing to lay back on their oars and do nothing. If any reward is due the man whose brain has produced something new and good he should get enough profits from the manufacture and sale of that thing." [8] Ford also held that the payment of cash royalties was wrong in principle, a view that may have been influenced by the "old Populist stuff" [9] that colored Ford's thinking. It is also probable that it was shaped as much by business acumen as by the contempt he had for the paper patent taken out by Selden.

"There is no power on earth, outside of the Supreme Court, which can make Henry Ford sign a license agreement or pay a royalty," boasted one of his patent attorneys.[10] This statement is only half-true. Since Ford had to make an accommodation to the patent system, there were occasions when he took out licenses and, as a last resort, even paid cash royalties. But the manner of that accommodation was consistent with the basic views he developed as a result of the Selden episode, and its ultimate effect, as a government official observed in 1938, was "just to abolish the patent system." [11]

As a rule, Ford adamantly refused to adopt parts and components patented by others. Instead, he ordered his engineers to evolve their own designs.[12] Only if they failed did the company take out a free license or a shop right. The company avoided payment of a cash royalty simply by using its massive economic power in an open market. For the ideas and devices that were the legal property of others, it traded the dispensation of its valuable contracts for the purchase of parts and materials. In many cases the parts-supplier who made a patented article for Ford also agreed to its manufacture by the Ford Motor Company in equal quantity on the basis of a free license or shop right. The profits made by the supplier on the Ford contract, as well as the assurance of sizable replacement orders from the vast army of Ford motorists, were the incentives to these arrangements.[13]

Here the company made a frank appeal to the realities of economic

[8] *The New York Times*, October 7, 1925.
[9] Welliver, "Henry Ford, Dreamer and Worker," p. 481.
[10] *The New York Times*, March 18, 1928.
[11] TNEC Hearings, Part 2: Patents, p. 331.
[12] Ernest G. Liebold to John F. Bible, November 17, 1922, Henry Ford Office Files, Accession 285, Box 84; Reminiscences of Lloyd Sheldrick, Oral History Section, Ford Archives.
[13] U. S. Circuit Court of Appeals for the Sixth Circuit: Ford Motor Company v. Parker Rust Proof Company, Transcript of Record on Appeal, II, 2192, 2193, 2200–2202; *The New York Times*, January 18, 1928; Vincent Bendix to C. E. Sorensen, July 5, 1929, Charles E. Sorensen Production Records, Accession 38, Box 114; J. Crawford to Edsel B. Ford, February 13, 1930, *ibid.*, Accession 38, Box 118; Reminiscences of J. L. McCloud and Theodore Gehle, Oral History Section, Ford Archives.

self-interest in a competitive business system where the rights vested in letters patent are worthless unless a market is created for the invention. Thus Ford, while remaining free of the automotive trade association and its patent pool, devised his own version of the cross-licensing agreement. Up to 1922, at least, the Ford Motor Company never paid a cash royalty to anyone for an outside patent used on the Ford car. It is significant that with only one known exception Ford made all of his agreements with actual producers.

Under this policy, the arts of negotiation and persuasion replaced the traditional usages of the patent system. Concomitantly, the company never prevented others from using patented inventions originated in its own laboratories or shops. "Since 1903," said a Ford spokesman in 1946,

> well over a thousand patents have been taken out by the Ford Motor Company. These patents have been licensed—innumerable times without charge—to businesses of all kinds and sizes. Ford recognizes the rights granted by patents, but rather than exact tribute for their use, believes that industry is best served when these rights are freely given, or traded for rights under patents owned by others.[14]

In this respect, Ford's commitment to free enterprise was absolute. Holding that too many patents were used to retard "the free use of ideas," he announced that his own patents would not be employed to curtail competition or to block the free flow of technological progress. "They will belong to the world," he said. "Anybody who wants to can use any improvement we make. The Ford organization has never proceeded against anybody for infringement of its patents." [15] Most of the Ford patents on the mechanical details of its automobiles were hardly as valuable as its patents on factory machinery and processes; and since the fertile technical resources and ingenuity of the Ford engineers were long unsurpassed in the industry, the flow of technological improvement was stimulated and enriched. In exchange for free licenses and shop rights, the Ford Company often taught its parts-suppliers how to raise their production efficiency, without reckoning its own investment in the experimental work that had developed new techniques.

The Ford Motor Company never used the infringement suit as an instrument of policy, although it is certain that its economic strength would have made it superior in most contests against lesser companies or individuals. It viewed the patent grant as a means of defense rather than of aggression, as a safeguard for its legitimate interests rather than a

[14] Gordon Fraser, "Ford Patents," Ford Sunday Evening Hour, March 24, 1946, American Broadcasting Company.

[15] William Atherton DuPuy, "If I Ran the Railroads—Ford," *Nation's Business*, IV (November 1921), 7–8.

tool for establishing monopolistic control. "We never intend using patents to stop anybody else (from) making our goods," said a high Ford official in 1919, "but we need them as a matter of defense and protection." [16] The company has never departed from this fundamental position.

In observing Independence Day in 1911, the year of its triumph over the Selden patent, the Ford Motor Company declared it had freed the automobile industry from "the straining fear of patent litigation and kindred evils." That boast became an actuality after other auto makers pondered the lessons of the Selden patent suit. Today the constructive results of that episode are embodied in the operations of an industry which for almost a half century has pioneered in diffusing the benefits of advanced technology. The patent policy of the Ford Motor Company and the cross-licensing agreement of other automobile producers are tantamount to radical surgery upon the body of the American patent system. Both patterns have preserved free technology along the frontiers of the automotive industry where conflicts over patent rights might well have hampered it.

[16] Ernest C. Kanzler to P. P. Barolin, March 20, 1919, Henry Ford Office Files, Accession 62, Box 109, Ford Archives.

14

Roger Burlingame:
"A Man Apart"[1]

The story of Henry Ford has been injured both by adulation and by equally mythical "debunking." It has often been written with only scant regard for the technical developments of his time and a failure to understand the workings of a mind whose concentration was primarily technical. Also, the myths on both sides have often stemmed from a desire to present a consistent picture—all black or all white—of a man for whom consistency in the constantly altering days in which he lived was obviously impossible. It is true that he was stubborn, hard to persuade, sometimes apparently quite madly erratic; yet it was his moments of flexibility, when he recognized—however reluctantly—the external pressures, that assured his ultimate success.

The "Ford-can-do-no-wrong" biographers insist upon the twin impulses of quantity and cheapness as a profound driving force that appeared with their hero's earliest consciousness and from which he never deviated. The debunkers point out many cases in which Ford completely departed from this line, such as when he forgot everything in his supposed passion for racing, when he designed and built several expensive models before his Model T, and when, even after Model T arrived and he stood on the very threshold of success, he seems to have been willing to sell out for cash. Both of these proponents are partly right and both are quite obviously, from the records available to us, partly wrong.

It is hard to deny that Henry Ford was ridden by two obsessions: mechanical perfection and the "common man." Sometimes one of these dominated the other. It is probable that in the years before Model T he was continuously searching for some sort of balance between the concentrations. Perhaps there were fleeting instants when the effort seemed too much for him. We can only guess at the inner workings of his mind, though it is possible that the immense volume of records he has left—only a fraction of which have been explored—will one day show more. In any

[1] From Roger Burlingame, *Henry Ford* (New York: Alfred A. Knopf, Inc., 1954), pp. 48–50, 56–58, 60–61, 81, 147–50, 177–79. Copyright © 1954 by Roger Burlingame. Reprinted by permission of Alfred A. Knopf, Inc. and Littauer and Wilkinson.

case, it is fatal to build the story of Henry Ford on any assumption other than that he was a human being subject to the pitfalls engendered by that peculiar quality we call genius.

* * *

We may put our finger precisely on 1907 as the year in which revolution came. It seems, looking back on it, as if fate played then into Ford's hands—as if it were a wind of destiny that shook the stock market in March, brought the most hopeful securities to the ground, and sowed the seeds of the October panic. The rich were hard hit. Low-priced cars were more than ever sought after. In the course of the year Ford production jumped to about eighty-five hundred, five times that of the previous year; and the great bulk of it consisted of the latest experimental light cars—Models N, R, and S, all selling for less than $1,000.

Watching these things, keeping careful track of costs, thinking of the future in terms of expansion beyond all dreams of the time in this first adolescence of the industry, Henry Ford evolved his great concept. It was in the light of this vision that he felt too confined in the Piquette-Beaubien plant, to which the company had moved when Strelow's Mack Avenue shop would no longer hold it. He planned for the purchase of the sixty-acre Highland Park race track, where he talked of building "the largest automobile factory in the world."

Various employees of the Ford Motor Comapny have claimed credit for the revoluntionary idea. It has been said that it was not one man's brainstorm, but the result of the focusing of many minds. It is undoubtedly true that others contributed details of design and, especially, production methods. But no one can examine the records or analyze the reminiscences of Ford workers of the period without knowing beyond question not only that Henry Ford's was the master mind but that the whole of the broad project originated with him. Indeed, we find evidence of discontented and sometimes angry rumblings throughout the time when the plan was taking shape and, indeed, of the disgusted exit of two of the most important production men in the plant. And with Ford's contemplation of the new gigantic installations at Highland Park—to be financed entirely by the plowing back of profits—the waves of unrest spread out to the stockholders. So the project had far from unanimous support.

* * *

Walter E. Flanders, machinist and production engineer, Ford's production manager from 1905 to 1908, thought the Model T project was impossible. He did not think the Model T itself was impossible. He was willing to try that. But he thought the *project* would be fatal to the company. He thought Ford was crazy to pursue it and said so. He then walked out before Ford had a chance to invite his departure.

It was not Ford's determination to produce Model T—a simple, sturdy, utilitarian, low-priced job—that worried Flanders. It was his determination *to produce nothing but.* It was a profound obsession in the industry that no manufacturer could survive concentrating on a single model—that he must offer a choice and make annual changes. Today we may sympathize with this view. The industrialists of 1907 were merely thinking twenty years ahead of their time. Mass production of this highly complex machine had to be established first—not only technically but economically as well. We know that a Model T project had to be injected into American society before the universal market and the universal desire could become facts. The *flexible* mass production that engineers are dreaming of in the 1950's will probably follow more flexible tastes of the future. But *inflexible* mass production had to precede it: neither the techniques nor the popular demand of the years immediately following 1907 would have permitted anything else. That was the fact: but of all the eager folk who were then engaged in pushing the horse off the American road, only Henry Ford knew it.

*　*　*

Later it was said that all Ford workers did not in fact get the minimum wage, that work was increased to a point where it turned hundreds of workers into nervous wrecks, and that the assembly lines had been speeded up to the point of nightmare. Like so many of the stories, good or bad, that were told about this fabled company, these reports were often exaggerated. Engineers who have studied large moving assembly complexes know, for instance, that to speed up a main assembly you have to speed up a dozen subassemblies at the same time and that some of them are not subject to quickening. Acceleration must, therefore, be gradual— not an overnight performance, as was charged. Also, every industrial engineer knows that sudden speed-ups result in expensive spoiled work. Nevertheless, that creeping, endless conveyor belt with its line of growing chassis inevitably lends itself to the picture, and the picture is difficult to erase.

*　*　*

More than any other single man, it was Henry Ford who made it possible for the United States to become the "arsenal of democracy" in the Second World War. This was not because of the contribution of Ford Motor Company plants to military production in that war. Theirs was only one of many. It was because through the manufacture of twenty million cars over some forty years Ford had evolved a certain pattern for all large-scale production including that of the atomic bomb.

The beautiful detail of this system was designed by engineers of the stature of Charles Sorensen, Peter Edward Martin, and William Knudsen and developed by a host of technicians and craftsmen. But the creative impulse, the direction, and the command, the selection of method and the elimination of nonessentials, and finally, the relentless drive, were one man's contribution. This might be called the art rather than the science of mass production. It was Henry Ford's gift to the world. In the five years following 1940 it brought success to the arms he hated but the military victory went, after all, to a coalition most of whose members believed in their various ways that they were fighting for freedom.

The elements of the Ford revolution were a century and a half old. The idea of making the parts of machines interchangeable so that the machines could be assembled at random was first put into practice by Eli Whitney in 1798. From the crude muskets he made on that plan through the classic sequence of the Colt revolver, the McCormick harvester, the Singer sewing machine, and the Pope bicycle, the plan had become more and more coordinated. But Henry Ford gave it a new form.

The essence of that form was motion and continuity. The moving assembly line changed the whole of the former structure. It set the pace for all the moving subassembly lines that came, at an angle, into it. Once that long conveyor started moving, everything in the factory had to move and move continuously. Every part of the motorcar had to be made at once so as to be ready at the right moment to take its place on the chassis.

So far, however, the Ford plan could not have created either the magnitude or the pace of American production in World War II. It could turn out cars with unprecedented speed. But until the entire nation became the factory, the scale would be inadequate. By 1940 this had become a possibility. By then the Ford Motor Company had long since burst the seams of any plant. Once upon a time assembly and subassemblies had been contained in Highland Park. Now even the great Rouge contained only a fraction of the operation. The subassemblies, with their lines of machines feeding into the chassis line, were no longer compact in a set of buildings. They were in cities wide apart, scattered from coast to coast. Parts could be made anywhere, assembled somewhere else. The long-established Ford practice of making parts in Dearborn for a car to be assembled, say, in Copenhagen was subject to infinite expansion.

By 1940 the Ford revolution had spread through all the automotive industry. General Motors, Chrysler, Packard, Willys—every manufacturer had taken over the Ford techniques entirely and added new ones in accord with the great pattern. It had affected many other kinds of manufacture. Its decentralizing possibilities had been eagerly seized upon in England, where the "bits and pieces" plan was well adapted to the short hauls in transportation and the multitude of small machine shops.

The final achievement of the Ford revolution, however, was the total isolation of the worker's mind. This has been bitterly and perhaps rightly attacked by sociologists, but it made possible the secrecy with which the atomic bomb and certain other weapons were produced. An assembly-line worker had by 1940 become wholly divorced from his end product. There was no longer any connection between his tightening of a single bolt and the motor car driving off the line thirty operations away. If, instead of an automobile, a tank, a tractor, or a three-inch gun had come off the line it would have made no difference to the man whose sole job was to tighten a bolt. With the same workmen any of these machines could have come off the line and, in the wartime, did.

This meant that a worker could do his job without knowing what he was making or why the man next to him did what he did. Thus it became possible to employ thousands of people in the production of a secret weapon without the purpose of their work ever becoming known to any of them. This could not have been done in the First World War. It was possible in the Second only because the Ford revolution, with all its far-reaching consequences, had intervened.

*   *   *

One of the primary causes of the failure to get at the true character of Henry Ford is the difficulty of divorcing the facts as they are recorded from the "Ford legend." Other captains of industry had practiced every sort of devious dealings and condoned shocking labor and business relations. The public, hearing of them, had simply nodded: sure enough, such things go on in business; it is too bad, but what can you expect? The targets were really not worthwhile for the critics to hit; the stories may have been bad enough, but they were not news. Ford, on that day in 1914 when he established a so-called minimum wage of five dollars for eight hours, acquired a halo that transformed him into the perfect target for all the "realists" and debunkers. From that moment until long after he was dead he was always news.

His own avowed belief was that the wage raise was simply good business. See, said the critics, what Ford does is hypocrisy; it pretends philanthropy, but actually it is simply good business! It was then the custom to do intensive research into Saint Henry's other hypocrisies. He speeded up assembly. He put a six-month qualification clause into the five-dollar minimum—a worker did not get it the day he was hired. So

Saint Henry resorted to the devious operation of firing men and rehiring them!

Anyone who had done so radical a thing was fair game for investigation. It was found that he censored the enriched workers' conduct off duty. A five-dollar man must be a moral man, thrifty, sober. This too was good business. Actually, spying on private lives was not peculiar to the Ford company. And the high-handedness of the company police who came later was nothing to that in Aliquippa or Ambridge or Wheeling or Weirton. But Ford must not do these things.

In an ironic article in the *American Mercury* for July 1931 Murray Godwin remembers the denunciation by critical writers of Ford's unloading his cars on the dealers in order to raise the money to repay his bank loan.

Ford raised the money (Godwin says) by arbitrary methods but at least he gave equally saleable goods as security. What if he had lost control (to the bankers)? Within a month or two a mountain of Ford stock would have burdened the country. The present depression would have come sooner and might have been more ruinous.

It was usually recognized that the world of big business was a world apart; that apparently ruthless decisions were often made to avoid large catastrophes. Sometimes there were large injustices, big concerns swallowed little ones, enormous concentrations of power grew up. The liberal journals cried out against these things and a good many people shook their heads about the "tycoons" who did them, but the events were rarely worth more than half a column in the daily press. But Ford was a man apart. He had set himself apart, true enough. A great concert of people, seeing his apartness, canonized him. To the rest he was the incarnate devil—not because of what he did, but against the background of his alleged sainthood. The dichotomy makes the post-mortem analysis—or synthesis—a complex task.

15

Allan Nevins and Frank E. Hill: "The Most Spectacular Career in American Industrial History" [1]

No informed man could doubt that Henry Ford's resignation closed perhaps the most impressive and certainly the most spectacular career in American industrial history. Nor could anyone doubt that his worldwide fame had been built on solid and enduring foundations. He had established the Ford Motor Company in 1903 as a daring venture in which few men dared embark their capital. After years of grueling struggle, making one successful car after another, the best labelled A, N, and S, his mechanical genius had produced the Model T, which precisely filled a ravenous national want. The insatiable demand for his automobile enabled him to erect at Highland Park one of the most shining, well-planned, and efficient factories on the globe. It enabled him and his associates to evolve there the magic instrument of industrial fecundity termed mass production; a magic still little understood, for many people equate it with quantity production, which is only one of its half-dozen leading components, but a process which has altered the world, and particularly America. From the early profits of the Model T and mass production bloomed the five-dollar day, which the London Economist has called the greatest single step in the history of wages.

The five-dollar day embodied a simple but inspired formula for the renovation of the economic and social life of industrialized nations. Mass production meant an opulence of manufactured goods; steady price reduction on these goods meant enlarged consumption, profits, and wage-paying capacity; and higher wages meant increased buying power to maintain the cycle. Once its efficacy was demonstrated, the formula seemed as obvious as Columbus' method of making the egg stand on end. Until it was tested it appeared so unworkable that most manufacturers thought it grotesque, and Ford had to battle his partner Malcomson before he could give it a trial. Ultimately it became the drive-wheel of the

[1] From Allan Nevins and Frank E. Hill, *Ford: Decline and Rebirth, 1932–1962* (New York: Charles Scribner's Sons, 1963), pp. 269–72. Copyright © 1962, 1963 by Columbia University. Reprinted by permission of Charles Scribner's Sons.

affluent society. People might say that the Model T was a happy mechanical accident, that mass production was the creation of many ideas and talents working in unison, and that the five-dollar day was a sudden impulsive decision; but genius went into each of these achievements, and the genius was Henry Ford's. It was the genius that his close and by no means uncritical associate Dean Marquis called a "supernormal perceptive faculty."

The Henry Ford who became not only world famous, but a world force, before 1915, was on the whole an attractive figure. Complex, wayward, mercurial, with a streak of meanness engendered by his hard early life, and prejudices that arose from ignorance, he could in spite of his glaring faults be called an idealist. He proved his interest in the workers not only by high wages but by making Highland Park and later the Rouge almost model plants in brightness, cleanliness, good air, and safety; still more by the thoughtful if sometimes overstrict welfare work of his Sociological Department. He proved his hatred of monopoly by his overthrow of the Selden patent, and continued to demonstrate it by making his patents and processes free to all. He proved his hatred of war, "a habit, and a filthy habit," by his Peace Ship, which he hoped might help end the insane butchery in Europe. His interest in schools and educational institutes, which he endowed in England, the South, and Michigan; his zeal in developing his industrial museum and Greenfield Village in Dearborn; his efforts to promote better agriculture and wholesome habits in recreation; his devotion to George Washington Carver and Martha Berry; his labors to demonstrate the social value of "village industries"— these showed facets of a true idealism. The Ford who loved old machines, old folksongs, old schoolbooks, and old dances, who built winter shelters for rabbits and grew corn for crows, who detested snobbery and class lines, and who was contemptuous of money, was thoroughly likable. It is not strange that Americans devoured books on him, and that Russian moujiks and Turkish mechanics wove wistful dreams about his name.

The years hardened him; his worse side wrestled more frequently with the better, until, after paralytic strokes lamed his mind, it seemed to master him. But responsibility for the change rested partly with his environment, with scheming and malicious men, and with changing times. Because rural Michigan of the 1870's had denied him a proper education, his ignorance laid him open to the lamentable suspicions of his anti-Semitic campaigns. The same ignorance, and the influence of reactionary men, made him a victim later of ideas fiercely hostile to government regulation, to New Deal reforms, and to organized labor. Meanwhile, the milk of his idealism had been curdled by cynical or spiteful attacks. Many American newspapers, he once burst out, were outrageously unfair. "They misquoted me, distorted what I said, made up lies." Part

of the press gibed at his Peace Ship beyond all warrant; business reaction-
aries had cast base aspersions on his motives in lifting wages to five dollars
a day; politicians and editors had made blackguardly attacks on Edsel as
an alleged draft dodger. The ridicule which accompanied the trial of his
libel suit against the *Chicago Tribune* would have seemed degrading to even
a less sensitive man. Then, too, the 1920's were unquestionably crasser
and more conservative than the preceding era, and the change in atmos-
phere affected him.

After the stroke of 1938 the old idealism showed itself only in rare
flashes, the old kindliness and philanthropy in few words and fewer deeds.
His hostility to labor, his surrender of plant control to hardfisted men,
his comradeship with Bennett, the countenance he gave to violence and
injustice, and above all, his tragic persecution of his own son, placed him
in a melancholy light. The growing senility of his last years was so carefully
concealed that people failed to make due allowance for it. But as he now
moved off the stage, tolerant observers knew that his career would have
to be viewed as a whole, and that in judging his darkened later years the
creative decades could not be forgotten. In perspective, those decades
counted far the most, and would be remembered when much that followed
was forgotten.

16
John Kenneth Galbraith: "A Relentless and Avid Self-Advertiser"[1]

The problem posed by Nevins and Hill, and by all the Ford literature, is that Ford is presented as a genius—an eccentric genius to be sure—who fails to reveal his genius even on the matters where it is supposed to be sublime. The nature of Ford's greatness has been variously identified. Crowther and likewise William J. Cameron, long familiar as the Sunday night voice of Ford on the radio, credited their employer with total social, economic, political, and philosophical insight. This view was widely accepted. Ford's social insights—those that led him to high wages and the five-dollar day and to the social benefits of mass production—are still very much a part of the myth.

Edison, who at first did not like Ford but later became his friend, is quoted as saying that "Ford is a 'natural businessman' just as he is a 'natural mechanic,' and he is the rarest of all types, in that he is a combination of the two." Certainly it is believed that Ford was the greatest business figure of his age and his mechanical genius is all but unchallenged. Nevins and Hill, who are more cautious about the qualifications of their hero than most, think his mechanical ability was beyond compare.

But if Ford had such vast endowments in these different fields, why was his performance in each marked by obtuseness and stupidity and, in consequence, by a congeries of terrible errors, many of them later admitted? Let us examine the record, beginning with Ford's performance as a political and social leader and as a philosopher.

In politics Ford was erratic and incompetent and, despite his vast industrial reputation, a disastrous failure. In 1918 he ran for the Senate on the Democratic ticket; and in 1924 he was, for a time, bitten by the presidential bug. Neither of these forays did anything to disprove his own candid observation that "about politics as a business I know nothing at

[1] From John Kenneth Galbraith, *The Liberal Hour* (Boston: Houghton Mifflin Company, 1960), pp. 149–52, 155–56, 162–65. Copyright © by John Kenneth Galbraith. Reprinted by permission of the Houghton Mifflin Company and John Kenneth Galbraith.

all," or the acid suggestion of *The New York Times* that his election in 1918 "would create a vacancy both in the Senate and in the automobile business." In his campaign Ford made no speeches, most likely because he could not speak. His most memorable contribution to political thought was the hint that, if elected Senator, he would take the Ford organization to Washington to help him. Reminded during his senatorial campaign of an earlier boast that he had rarely bothered to vote, he let it be known that in 1884, just turned twenty-one, he had gone promptly to the polls and on his father's advice marked his ballot for President Garfield. That was three years after Garfield was assassinated. (Ford had other such accidents. From the peace ship went a cable to Pope Benedict VII, who died in 983.) In this campaign Ford was for Wilson and the League of Nations. But this alignment with the angels must be set against later flirtations with such unrewarding figures as Father Coughlin, Fritz Kuhn, and Gerald L. K. Smith.* And common political shrewdness, if nothing else, would have warned him against *The Protocols of the Wise Men of Zion*, a notorious forgery, and the other racial rubbish that month after month appeared in the *Dearborn Independent*, along with Mr. Ford's own page, and which blamed the Jews for all man's sins and most of his misfortunes since Moses. When, in the end, the popular, commercial, and legal objections to this farrago became overpowering, Ford set a new standard for audacious falsehood by denying that he had had anything to do with it. "Had I appreciated even the general nature, to say nothing of the details, of these utterances, I would have forbidden their circulation without a moment's hesitation." [2] The denial was not only bogus but foolish. Every person whose knowledge counted knew that Ford had been specifically and personally responsible.

*   *   *

Neither was Henry Ford a businessman. On this the evidence is decisive, and if there is any uncertainty as to what a businessman is, he is assuredly the things Ford was not.

Ford paid no attention to questions of company organization—there usually wasn't much after Couzens left—or to administration, costs, marketing, customer preference, or (at least by his own assertion) profits. The older executives at the Ford Motor Company agree that power was not delegated but appropriated. In the late thirties and early forties, Harry Bennett carried this technique to the logical conclusion by basing his authority on armed force. Balance sheets and cost accounts meant nothing to Henry Ford. Neither did his dealer organization, although

---

* [All three led organizations with strong leanings toward Naziism—ed.]

[2] From Ford's retraction in 1927 following settlement of his lawsuit with Aaron Sapiro. Quoted in Nevins and Hill, *Expansion and Challenge*, p. 321.

when Model T ceased to sell, he blamed it on the dealers. One of his contributions to the merchandising of Ford cars was to ban advertising for several years. Some will insist that he had the greatest of all business talents, which was a sure feel for what the customer wanted. Perhaps he did, but not reliably so. In the twenties, he failed to see that people, new car buyers at least, wanted a more comfortable and elegant car than he was providing and would pay for it. He stuck with the Model T and surrendered the leadership of the industry to General Motors. He is remembered for saying that the customers could have Model T in any color "so long as it is black." This was refreshing individualism and so much a part of Ford's character that Will Rogers, taking cognizance of Ford's presidential ambitions in the early twenties, offered him an unbeatable slogan: "Voters, if I'm elected, I'll change the front." But it was supreme indifference to those he was supposed to serve, and it nearly ruined the company.

*　　*　　*

What, then, is the answer? For it still remains that Henry Ford built the most famous car of all time, certainly the greatest manufacturing enterprise of its day. In an age when so many men are subject to the expansive and expensive attentions of public relations experts, debunking should perhaps be subsidized. But the debunker operates on the phony— the man whose accomplishments are confined to the press releases. Ford's accomplishments are there for all to see. How did a man with such grievous shortcomings do (or become identified with) so much?

One reason is that because the Ford was the first car most people ever knew, Ford is awarded honors as an inventor he did not entirely deserve. He built and drove his first horseless vehicle in 1896, although not un-characteristically, in what Nevins calls a blend of "poor memory and wishful thinking," he later made the date "about 1891 and 2." By 1896 dozens of boys and men had done or were doing the same thing. And some had done far more than Ford. The automobile, as Merz* and doubtless others have said, was not invented. Engine and chassis were developed over a period of years. Ford was a latecomer. Four years before he wheeled out his car for its dramatic (and subsequently much publicized) midnight run in Detroit, the firm of Panhard and Levassor in Paris had *issued a catalog* of their line of gasoline-powered cars. Things were less advanced in America—the gasoline buggy which the Duryea brothers drove in 1892 in Springfield, Massachusetts, was far more primitive than the French vehicles—but both they and others were far ahead of Ford.

Ford did build several early cars and made something of a name for

---

* Charles Merz, author of *And Then Came Ford* (Garden City, N. Y., 1929).

himself as a racer. These were considerable achievements, although others did as much who never acquired his reputation. Much of the early difference was almost certainly made by a group of able men—Couzens, Wills and the Dodge brothers—who joined Ford in the early years of the century to have the benefit of his public name. It is to Ford's credit that he accepted their help. But it would be hard to say whether he selected them or they selected him.

The company made money from the first year. Its cars were no better and no cheaper than those of its competitors, and this was long before the arrival of Model T. In the success of the Ford Motor Company, something must be credited to the indiscriminate enthusiasm with which people bought automobiles. No invention so nearly sold itself. At first Ford did not see any special advantage in a cheap, light car, but later when he did he seized upon it with unequaled tenacity. That Ford was a tenacious man, none can doubt. Then it did him a great service. Later it did him equal disservice.

The Model T when it arrived in 1908 was not mechanically ahead of its time nor was it especially inexpensive. But supporting Ford's undoubted conviction that this was the right car were the talents of one of the great organizers of all times—James Couzens. He created the superb dealer organization which sold and serviced the cars. This produced an insistent pressure on the factory and then he organized the production that sought to supply the demand. Ford did not interfere; in these days of almost incredible expansion before the First World War he spent little time at the factory. Sorensen has called these years the "Couzens Period." "Everyone in the company, including Henry Ford, acknowledged his as the driving force during this period." [3] In contrast with Ford, Couzens never gave a sign of being impressed by his achievement.

After Couzens left in 1915, Ford took full command, and the company was never so successful again. It was partly the prestige and fame which success had brought to his name which caused Ford to assume control, and Couzens resigned partly because he felt that Ford wished to use the business as his personal advertisement. In the years that followed, Ford was a relentless and avid self-advertiser. And he mobilized the efforts of many others to promote not the car but the man. Only the multitude remained unaware of the effort which Ford, both deliberately and instinctively, devoted to building the Ford myth. He seemed such an unassuming man. He was the first and by far the most successful product of public relations in industry.

Finally, a word can be said in explanation of at least some of his mistakes. Ford was born in 1863. He emerged as a national figure in

[3] *My Forty Years with Ford*, p. 36.

1914, the year of the five-dollar day, when he was fifty-one. Many of the mistakes which contradict his claim to stature were made after that. Any reasonable view of Ford must reckon with the fact that, in the years when the light beat hardest upon him, he was past his prime. Success had made him immune to counsel and advice; for too long he had seen eccentricity and even mere foolishness pictured as genius and had believed it.

17

R. L. Bruckberger:
"The Ford Revolution"[1]

The difficulty in evaluating Henry Ford is that most of his methods, in his own country at least, have been so generally adopted that people no longer realize how enormously original they were and how extraordinarily fruitful they have been. Nowadays, we have an unfortunate tendency to remember only Ford's personal eccentricities and that hardness of his which so marked the last years of his life. But in 1912 he was not yet fifty and had only recently become the head of an enterprise which so impressed an Irish writer that he said, "When you study the Ford Company, you have before you a great State, perfect in every particular—the nearest that anything on the face of the earth has got to Utopia." Such a comment proves how revolutionary Ford appeared to his contemporaries.

Henry Ford was born in 1863 on a farm near Detroit. His father, an immigrant of peasant stock, fully intended that his eldest son should also stay on the land, and in fact Henry Ford did not definitely give up farming to become a mechanic until 1891, when he was twenty-eight. For the rest of his life this background was to give him a Puritan asceticism, a strong feeling for nature and solitude, for trees and birds, together with a truly revolutionary determination to lighten the farmer's burden of toil and someday ease his fate. This he achieved, more than anyone else in the world.

Yet his true vocation, the only thing he loved, was machinery. His schoolwork had been mediocre, and he never lost his contempt for books. The strength of his genius—for he had genius—lay in his passion for anything mechanical, for any kind of machine, from the movement of a watch to a locomotive. Later he was to say of his childhood years, "My toys were all tools—they still are." And again he said, "Machines are to a mechanic what books are to a writer. He gets ideas from them and, if he

---

[1] From R. L. Bruckberger, *Image of America* (New York: The Viking Press, 1959), pp. 181–83, 184–85, 186–88, 193–94, 195–97, 201–2. Copyright © 1959 by R. L. Bruckberger. Reprinted by permission of The Viking Press and Harold Matson Co., Inc.

has any brains, he will apply those ideas." He was a born mechanic; he was never anything else but a mechanic, an inventor in mechanics. This was both his strength and his limitation. The social upheaval which Edison believed to be necessary, the emancipation of worker and peasant for which Marx longed, Ford also kept constantly in mind. But he was convinced that the machine itself, the increase of mechanization, could at least make possible, if it could not actually bring about, that upheaval and that emancipation. Today it is obvious that all the countries in the world are attempting to industrialize themselves, that Russia's prestige among backward nations derives less from its Marxism than from its industrial achievement, and that true national independence is no longer conceivable without industrialization. But if this is now self-evident, it was less so in 1889, when Henry Ford announced to his bewildered young wife that he was going to build a horseless carriage, that horses were obsolete, and that within a few years horseless carriages would jam New York's Fifth Avenue. Oddly enough, Henry Ford always detested horses, and it seems that his feeling was reciprocated.

In any wholly new undertaking there is a long period of growth between the germ of the idea and its fruition. On Christmas night, 1893, in the kitchen of his Detroit home and with the help of his wife, Henry Ford successfully tested his first internal-combustion engine. In 1896 he put an engine in his first quadricycle. He did not sell his first automobile until 1903, when he was forty years old. And it was only some ten years later, after he had brought out his Model T, expanded his factories, integrated production and distribution, and made the famous decision to pay his workers five dollars for an eight-hour day, that Ford realized his lifelong ambition and won both fame and fortune. Until then no one but his wife had really believed in his genius. The story goes that when he built his first automobile and drove proudly home to the farm, his father received him coldly. No doubt the old farmer felt that a man of thirty-three with a family, who left his grocer's bills unpaid for three months, had better things to do than waste time and money toying with mechanical contraptions.

*   *   *

Certain words may sound absurd and even distasteful when applied to industry, yet one cannot avoid using them. While Ford's stockholders thought of the company strictly in terms of profit and loss, he envisioned its role as essentially apostolic and missionary. Success soon proved the truth of the idea. Ford actually thought of himself as a kind of Saint Paul, charged with the burden and anxious care, not of all the churches, but of all the regions of the world, sending out to all peoples everywhere, not epistles, but automobiles, trucks, tractors, and engines; carrying to every nation of the earth, not a message of supernatural hope, but a promise of progress and liberation. Henry Ford considered himself, and was, prophet and apostle of the machine, its witness and its martyr. Such a conviction, held with such intensity, offended, shocked, and profoundly disturbed the purely mercenary temper of the capitalist world. According to the most deeply rooted, the most revered, the absolutely sacrosanct bourgeois tradition, prophets and apostles can be tolerated as quaint epiphenomena of civilization, but one must never, never in the world, bring them into a meeting of the board of directors.

Henry Ford was not only on the Board of Directors of his company but also ran the company and managed and organized its factories. He was determined to make it serve his prophetic vision. Inevitably, he was not understood; inevitably, there was conflict. Whatever the impact and success of their message, prophets live and die alone. The loneliness and intransigence of those last years which caused Henry Ford to make so many sorry mistakes stemmed not only from his obstinacy and pride but also from his conviction that he had always been able to see what others had failed to see, what others had consistently refused to see, and from his feeling that for so long, against everyone and quite alone, he had been right.

*　　*　　*

If I am to say where money stood in the scale of Henry Ford's values, I say it stood last. First came work, and man's power, through work, to create. In work Ford saw life's joy and purpose. Work was not a livelihood; work was life itself. "Thinking men," he wrote, "know that work is the salvation of the race, morally, physically, socially. Work does more than get us our living; it gets us our life." As a true Puritan, Ford was essentially a moralist, and again as a true Puritan, he reduced all morality to the practice of a single virtue—work. Just as the devout Christian finds the highest expression of his faith in martyrdom, so Henry Ford found the most perfect expression of man's labor and productivity in industry, and held it to be sacred and honorable. He had no use for art, and in that, too, he was a true Puritan.

Ford saw, however, and as clearly as Marx, that certain conditions of work can degrade rather than ennoble. We remember Marx's well-known statement on the "degrading distinction between intellectual and manual labor." I do not suppose this statement would have made much sense to Ford, had he come upon it, for he had long since reconciled any such distinction in himself. Essentially he was a man who had always worked with his hands, first on a farm, then in a factory. He had never ceased to be a mechanic, yet at the same time he had always been a reflective man— a thinker, if you will, and why not? Indeed, he even claimed that his years of manual labor, his passion for tools and the raw material they transform, did more to sharpen his intelligence than books ever could for self-styled intellectuals. In Ford's view, manual labor led—by a path different from that of intellectual or artistic intuition, but just as directly, just as surely—to the fulfillment of what Simone Weil has so superbly called "the original pact of the mind with the universe."

Ford had the zeal of an apostle. It was not enough for him to have solved a problem to his own satisfaction; he wanted to bring his solution to the entire world. Upon close examination, the whole originality of Ford's discovery consists in his penetrating and thoroughly practical vision of the vast role that mechanization can play in emancipating human society. Long ago Aristotle foresaw that the development of the machine would one day make it possible to abolish slavery and that a time would come when men ceased to enslave other men and had "mechanical slaves" instead. Henry Ford carried out Aristotle's prophecy, and did it deliberately, too. This is what made him great; this is what made him infinitely more revolutionary than Marx, who was only an intellectual. The Russians obviously understood this, since they sent their engineers to be trained in Ford's factories and requested Ford engineers for Russia. Time after time, and even as a young man, Henry Ford spoke with unmistakable clarity about the emancipation that the machine would bring. "The machine and not the man," he wrote, "would be the drudge." It was imperative, he said, "to lift . . . drudgery off flesh and blood and lay it on steel and motors."

The linking of Henry Ford to Aristotle leads to even wider implications. Aristotle accepted slavery because it benefited a minority of free men, relieving them of servile tasks and enabling them to consecrate their lives to philosophy, art, and the government of the republic. There was no other base for an aristocratic society except slavery. But Henry Ford saw that if the burden of slavery were shifted from man to the machine, there would be time for leisure and creativity for all mankind, and that therefore the development of machinery would tend to create its own aristocratic society, for, although society is based on the dialectic of master and slave, with the advent of the machine all men can become masters. Thus, through the mastery of nature, man will at last be reconciled to man. Needless to say, this is an optimistic and visionary view. Experience has taught us that the machine also creates oppressions, and Ford was fully aware of it. Yet I firmly believe that this optimistic and visionary view was his and that he devoted his life to the attempt to realize it.

* * *

From the start, Ford's contemporaries realized the full import of this revolution in production. Clearly, it meant the end of the craftsman and of manufacture by hand. It meant the end of a kind of luxury. It meant the end, or at least a postponement, of any preoccupation with esthetics in manufacturing; it meant the enthronement of monotony. In 1950, when I arrived for the first time in New York, a young American who spoke excellent French took me on a tour of the city. After some hours, he became aware that I was tired and possibly somewhat disappointed. "I admit none of this is as picturesque as Spain, or Greece or Italy," he said, abruptly. "But to us Americans, the picturesque is other people's squalor." Now, after eight years in America, I still remember what he said. No one else has helped me to understand America so well. When Henry Ford put America on wheels, he rescued the farmer from his isolation and brought him within reach of railroads to carry his produce to New York or San Francisco and carry back machines and city goods. By bringing the market to the farmer's door as Henry C. Carey [American economist (1793–1879), called by Bruckberger "the only American economist of importance"—ed.] had envisioned, Ford created an unlimited national market. He opened up an immense hinterland rich in untapped resources. He brought the newspaper to every isolated farmer from the Atlantic to the Pacific. Thanks to him, it soon became possible for everyone to get to the motion pictures. He had breached a solitude. One does not sacrifice such a gift of freedom to the esthetic value of a piece of hand-woven silk.

*   *   *

How I wish I could find words to impress the reader with the importance of that decision of the five-dollar day! It meant infinitely more than a mere raise in wages. The "timing," to use the vernacular of the theatre, was a stroke of genius, for the five-dollar day not only undermined the whole capitalist structure but cut away the ground from under Marxist revolution. Let me speak plainly: I consider that what Henry Ford accomplished on January 1, 1914, contributed far more to the emancipation of workers than the October Revolution of 1917. The Revolution of Lenin and his colleagues, however bloody, was still only a literary revolution which never emerged from the mythical political economy invented by Ricardo and Marx. The fact is that Lenin's Revolution was bloody precisely because it was literary. But Henry Ford, in his characteristically American way, cared nothing for mythical or literary revolution. Having covered his blackboard with figures, he moved straight into "truth and reality." What Marx had dreamed, Ford achieved. But he achieved it only because he was far more of a revolutionary than Marx or Lenin. Ford exploded the whole idea of the famous, supposedly immutable "iron law" of wages on which Ricardo believed capitalist economy was founded and which was to provide every proletarian revolution with a springboard.

Like Lincoln in answer to Karl Marx, Ford avoided rhetoric. "The payment of five dollars a day for an eight-hour day," he was to explain, "was one of the finest cost-cutting moves we ever made." And he added, "Well, you know when you pay men well, you can talk to them." Yet he knew exactly what he was doing; he knew exactly how revolutionary he was. "I can find methods of manufacturing," he said, "which will make high wages the cheapest of wages . . . if you cut wages, you just cut the number of your own customers." Customer—that is the key word, the key to Ford's social revolution, a revolution made not in fiction but in the reality of political economy. Just as Ford took the automobile out of the luxury class, made it inexpensive, and put it into the class of basic necessities, so, at his blackboard on January 1, 1914, he took the worker out of the class of the "wage-earning proletariat" to which Ricardo and Marx had relegated him and gave him new dignity as a customer. At one stroke he exploded the theory of the "minimum-subsistence wage" ("turning men into hats") so unjustly and so firmly established as a "law" of economics by Ricardo, so justly and so firmly denounced by Marx. He abolished the "minimum-subsistence wage"—"that price which is necessary to enable laborers, one with another, to subsist and perpetuate their race." He made every worker a potential customer.

Where is the honor, some may ask, where is the special human dignity in being a customer? I wish at this point that we Europeans would finally bury once and for all the historic prejudices we inherit from an essentially aristocratic and military concept of honor. In any case, social and economic questions are of a wholly different order, and in the economic order, with which Marx claimed to be so exclusively concerned, there is no doubt whatever that the word "customer" lends as much dignity as the word "citizen" lends in the political order of a free republic. A man is a customer on the market when he has purchasing power, just as he is a citizen of the republic when he has the power to influence affairs of state. In the last analysis, the customer controls the market and is therefore a free citizen of it. With Ford, the American worker became a customer, and in fact the best of customers. But one cannot be both a customer and a proletarian at the same time, any more than, at the same time and in the same equation, one can be both a master and a slave. The emancipation of the proletariat which Marx could only envisage as the result of a revolution that would "violently destroy the ancient order of production" was achieved by Ford, very simply, without fanfare, in front of a blackboard. In other words, and I shall return to this later, Ford transformed the ancient order of production without violence and yet more radically

than Lenin. He was as far outside the Ricardo-Marx dialectic as Carey.
Ford, too, was a man who was never bound by any form of Euclidian
postulate. Who would dare suggest today that American workers exist
only "in the guise of the most miserable class"? The change in the lot
of the workers is a tremendous fact that neither Ricardo nor Marx
foresaw.

*   *   *

There is, in all this, a great lesson, and that is what I am coming to.
The most spectacular side of Henry Ford's discoveries, the universal
application of assembly-line methods to the production and distribution
of goods—that specifically mechanical and industrial side of his discoveries—is, by its very nature, independent of the social system in which
it operates. As a matter of fact, Russia has also adopted Ford's industrial
technique, and this has probably done more to consolidate the Soviet
regime than Marx's absurd philosophy. Ford's technique is a highly
perfected tool for production and distribution, but, like all tools, it can
be handled by anyone. His industrial methods have neither nationality
nor ideology; they are equally effective in a totalitarian state or in a
democracy, just as psychoanalytic therapy is as effective in Paris or New
York as in Moscow.

Ford's methods were also to affect the structure of society. Let us
not forget how clearly he put this himself. "I can find methods of manufacturing," he said, "which will make high wages the cheapest of wages
. . . if you cut wages, you just cut the number of your own customers."
This is the essence of his contribution to social change, and that contribution was prodigious. Henry Ford broke the mainspring of capitalism and
Marxist revolution, as the mainspring of a watch is broken. After Ford,
the systems of capitalism and Marxist revolution were rendered as useless
as blunted and obsolete tools. Ford did no more than define his methods
and apply them. But this was enough to prove that Henry Charles Carey's
ideal of social harmony was eminently practical and practicable. Yet he
failed to follow Carey's thought to the end; he failed to see that the final
goal of all production must be to civilize, or rather he held too narrowly
material and mechanistic a view of civilization. He had no real understanding for "man in his highest aspirations" or for man's uncompromising
sense of personal dignity. But this the trade unionists of America were to
teach him.

18

Roger Butterfield:
Ford and History [1]

Ford's most discerning biographers have noted that the *Tribune* trial scarred his personality; that it "tinged his mind with wariness, bitterness, and cynicism." [2] It can also be said that he carried away from it a happy and fruitful new mission in life. Riding back from Mt. Clemens to Detroit, after the jury awarded him six cents in damages, Ford was neither abashed nor silent.

"We're going to start something," he told Ernest Liebold, his principal secretary. "I'm going to start up a museum and give people a true picture of the development of the country. That's the only history that is worth observing, that you can preserve in itself. We're going to build a museum that's going to show industrial history, and it won't be bunk." [3]

The concept of history as exhibits and objects, rather than words, was at least as old as the tombs of Egypt, but it seems to have struck Ford suddenly. Before 1919, when he talked about history, it was obvious he was referring to books, and especially schoolbooks, which he remembered, "began and ended with wars." [4] But during his ordeal on the witness stand Ford was forced to think about history, and he came up with some broad definitions. History included last week's airships, the growth of the country through industry, achievements with tools and machines.

After such notions were lodged in his mind Ford's interest in historical artifacts expanded very rapidly. He decided to collect "all American things—domestic and mechanical." He came as close to doing this as one man ever will. In 1931, only twelve years after Mt. Clemens, a professional historian reported that Ford's collections at Dearborn were then being arranged in five "impressive, dignified, in every way satisfying" new buildings, and that they were notable and voluminous in the follow-

---

[1] From Roger Butterfield, "Henry Ford, the Wayside Inn, and the Problem of 'History Is Bunk,' " *Proceedings of the Massachusetts Historical Society*, LXXVII (1965), 57–66. Reprinted by permission of the Massachusetts Historical Society.

[2] Nevins and Hill, *Ford*, p. 142.

[3] E. G. Liebold, "Reminiscences," p. 90, Ford Archives, Acc. 65 (Oral History, typed transcripts).

[4] *Detroit Free Press*, Sept. 6, 1915; *Tribune Suit Record*, p. 5659.

ing and other classifications: farm implements and machinery, mines and metallurgy, household and kitchen furniture, domestic utensils, costumes, recreation and amusements, lighting, spinning, weaving, sewing, trade and commerce, timekeeping, medicine and surgery, communication and record of ideas, music, photography, science, schools, taverns, peddlers and chapmen, maps and pictures, fire prevention, forestry and wood-working, horticulture, machine tool and shop practice, steam traction engines and, of course, transportation.[5]

Only one major activity of man was slighted—there were no weapons or mementos of war.

Wednesday, June 20th, 1923, was a red-letter day in Ford's collecting career. At 10:30 A.M. he left the Copley-Plaza Hotel in Boston and was driven out Route 20 in the direction of Worcester. With him were two of his favorite companions and Ford dealers, Gaston Plantiff from New York and Dutee Flint from Providence, and another man he had met recently, L. Loring Brooks, a Boston banker, who had an office at 53 State Street and a home, Sunset Ledge Farm, in Framingham. The four were en route to the ancient Red Horse tavern at South Sudbury, known since the publication of Longfellow's 1863 *Tales* as the Wayside Inn.[6]

Ford had decided to buy the Inn, which local enthusiasts claimed was the oldest in the United States. But his first tour through its rooms was discouraging. There was no old spinet with ivory keys, no somber clocr with maker's name, no firelight with its ruddy glow filling "the parlok large and low." As a matter of fact those things were not there when Longfellow wrote his "Prelude," either. The original proprietors, the Howe (or How) family, had closed the Inn before October 31, 1862, when Longfellow rode out to seek inspiration.[7] For years after that it stood abandoned, until it was bought in 1897 by Edward Lemon, an antiques collector. Under his management it was a popular resort for sleighing and cycling parties, artist members of Boston's Paint and Clay Club, and Universalist ministers, who held regional "retreats" there. Lemon died in 1919, his widow closed the Inn again.[8]

Ford looked over the situation thoughtfully. Not far from the Inn's

[5] J. G. de Roulhac Hamilton, "The Ford Museum," *American Historical Review*, XXXVI (July 1931), 772–75.

[6] L. Loring Brooks to Mr. and Mrs. Henry Ford, postmarked May 24, 1922; Brooks to Ford (unsigned memorandum), July 19, 1923; both in Ford Archives, Acc. 1, Box 84 (Fair Lane Papers).

[7] *Life of Henry Wadsworth Longfellow with Extracts from his Journals and Correspondence*, ed. Samuel Longfellow, 2 vols. (Boston, 1886), pp. 11, 388.

[8] "Wayside Inn History" (untitled typescript), pp. 52–55, Ford Archives, Acc. 1, Box 86; Lucia Ames Mead, "How The Old Wayside Inn Came Back," *Old-Time New England*, XXXII (July 1931), 41–45.

front door was a roadside shack labeled "Coffee Cup" which catered to a new kind of public, including drivers of Model T's. As Ford said later, the Inn was on a much-traveled highway, and "there was nothing at all to prevent it from being exploited and the roads lined for a half mile around by peanut and hot dog stands, and side shows, and all kinds of catch-penny places." [9] He drove around the neighborhood, stopping at homes and farms, and then authorized Brooks to obtain options to buy more than a dozen properties, "naming [a] sum to cover all."

Brooks completed most of this assignment during the next two weeks. But he could not reach a satisfactory agreement with a Mr. Peter Gannon, who owned a billiard parlor in Framingham, and announced that he planned to open a kennel of police dogs on the highway near the Inn. Gannon himself had only an option, recently acquired, for which he was asking $50,000, because—as he explained to Brooks—he expected to make $10,000 a year during the next five years by the sale of police dogs. "I told him," Brooks reported to Ford, "that I knew something about dogs, as I had had a kennel of Irish Terriers for some twenty-five years, and could not see any such income from dogs." [10]

Gannon capitulated to other Ford agents; in time the Wayside Inn property, with its affiliated farms and schools, spread over eighty-eight parcels of land, totaling 2,667 acres, in the towns of Sudbury, Framingham, and Marlborough. The roadside menace was disposed of in 1927 and 1928. Ford deeded eighteen acres to the Commonwealth of Massachusetts, with a request to move the road away from the Inn—an innovation in tavernkeeping that would surely have startled his predecessors. The road was removed and rebuilt, and Ford cheerfully paid the cost: $330,831.01. [11]

All this was merely mechanics; the expensive nuts and bolts of the project. Ford selected the Wayside Inn—out of a number of sites available—as a showcase, a kind of soapbox, and a working model for the much

[9] "Henry Ford: Why I Bought the Wayside Inn. An Interview with Samuel Crowther," *Country Life*, April, 1925, p. 44. "In October, 1897, the first automobile ever seen at the Inn made its appearance. It was a Stanley Steamer." "Wayside Inn History," p. 55.

[10] Brooks to Ford (unsigned memorandum), July 19, 1923. Brooks in 1922 was the prime mover in a campaign to save the Wayside Inn. With public endorsements from Charles W. Eliot, Henry Cabot Lodge, Mrs. Nathaniel Thayer, Dr. Myles Standish, Charles Francis Adams, B. Loring Young, and E. Sohier Welch, Brooks invited 200 "prominent persons throughout the United States" to become shareholders in a Wayside Inn Trust, the shares to cost $500 each. "The response given by Mr. Henry Ford . . . was the heartiest response of all" (and made further solicitation unnecessary). "Wayside Inn History," pp. 55–56; *Boston Transcript*, April 18, 1922; *Old-Time New England*, XII (April 1922), 175–76.

[11] "Re Wayside Inn, South Sudbury, Massachusetts," typed financial summary prepared in 1945 by L. J. Thompson, Ford Archives, Acc. 384.

bigger museum he was planning to build at Dearborn. Up to 1923 he collected only things, including a few colonial houses. But he had not yet evolved a suitable scheme for attracting and pleasing the American public, and winning it over to his version of history.

At the Wayside Inn he worked this out, in a way that profoundly affected historical guardianship in the United States. This was the first place where an individual, possessing all the money needed, set out to restore and put on display not just one famous building, but a sizable, functioning community of homes, farms, schools, craft industries, chapel, and village tavern—with the purpose, as Ford stated it, "to show how our forefathers lived and to bring to mind what kind of people they were." [12]

The results of his experiment were mixed, but the example he set began an era. Wayside Inn was the pilot project for all the museum villages and towns that swarm on the American landscape today.

It was also relaxing fun for Ford, who paid close attention to the details. The reports and letters he received on the Inn and its allied activities fill forty-two boxes in the tremendous Ford Archives at Dearborn. As soon as he received title to the Inn he sent a young man from his office, Frank Campsall, to scout its history and possibilities.

"Longfellow slept here at least one night—undoubtedly more—on the authority of his daughter Alice who slept in the smaller room adjoining his, as related by her to Mrs. Lemon," Campsall soon reported. He had also learned that James T. Fields, Longfellow's publisher, often slept in the third floor garret because "he liked to hear the rain come down on the roof." Campsall listed dates for various additions and outbuildings, ranging from "about 1800" to as late as 1915. He both dashed and raised Ford's hopes by saying he had not found the famous spinet, but that some "original pieces" were still owned by a Mr. Howe, a relative of the old-time innkeeper. "We will run over to see him some evening," he added.[13]

Apparently nothing came of this. In November the search for furniture was taking its predictable direction—to the Boston antiques experts. "Talked with Wallace Nutting yesterday," Campsall wrote, "and at first said nothing about his collection speaking generally about getting furniture to refurnish the Inn in period prior to 1700. He stated it could be done and would probably take about 6 months—Intimated that if you would give him a retainer of $2500.00 per year he would buy furniture in his name cheaper than we could."

Mr. Nutting was "pretty independent and of an artistic temperament," Campsall added. But he had arranged with Israel Sack, a prominent dealer, to withdraw a collection which was on loan at the art museum—

---

[12] "Henry Ford: Why I Bought the Wayside Inn," p. 44. Writers on the preservation movement have failed to give Ford his due.

[13] Campsall to Ford, July 15, 1923, Ford Archives, Acc. 1, Box 84.

"Sack called and stated that he was going to lay out and appraise so you can see it altogether—estimates roughly 45 to 50 M." Campsall was also after books. "Was over to Goodspeed's—the book man—and instructed him to ship in the early editions of Longfellow's books which he wrote us about. . . . Selected some children's books of the period 1840–80. . . . Had quite a chat with him and believe you would enjoy meeting him. Enquired about your statement 'History is bunk' and when I explained your meaning* agreed stating however that it should have been *Histories*."

Campsall was very busy by this time, supervising remodeling of the Inn, locating an ox sling for the blacksmith shop, and tracking down a "very early end brake hand tub" fire engine. But he took pains to arrange for one of his boss's favorite pastimes. "Have stopped up the pond by the ice house to raise it so you can have some skating a little later," he wrote.[14]

In the Ford Archives there is a little card, with a wisp of wool attached to its middle, and inscribed in an old lady's tremulous writing "Knitted yarn from the first fleece of Mary's Little Lamb. Mary E. Tyler. Somerville. Jan. 27, 1880." Ford received this in 1925, along with letters and printed matter which identified Mrs. Tyler as the original Mary of the famous poem. Her maiden name was Mary Sawyer; she was born in 1806 at Sterling, Massachusetts, and died in 1889. She had never claimed more than the first twelve lines of the poem. These were written and handed to her, she said, by a childhood admirer, John Roulstone, Jr., who watched the lamb follow her to school, in "about the year 1817."

Ford, accompanied by his wife, pursued this lead in person. They visited various places in Massachusetts and New Jersey, and interviewed members of the Sawyer and Tyler families. Ford established that there was indeed a John Roulstone, Jr., who lived in Sterling at the same time as Mary, and died in 1822, aged 17, while still a Harvard freshman. He learned that John Roulstone's father had been an officer of the Ancient and Honorable Artillery Company, that his portrait hung in Faneuil Hall, and his grave was in the Old Granary. Ford collected magazine articles and books, none written before 1890 and read in one of them a statement by Mary:

> From the fleece sheared from my lamb, mother knit two pairs of very nice stockings, which for years I kept in memory of my pet. But when the ladies were raising money for the preservation of the Old South Church in Boston, I was asked to contribute one pair of stockings for the benefit of the fund. This I did. The stockings were raveled out, pieces of the yarn being fastened to cards bearing my autograph, and these cards were sold, the whole realizing, I am told, about one hundred dollars. After the first

* Something Ford himself failed to do in 1919! [R. B.]
[14] Campsall to Ford, November 21, 1923, Ford Archives, Acc. 1, Box 84.

pair were thus sold, the ladies wanted more yarn; and they were so anxious to have the other pair . . . that I gave them also. Now all I have left in remembrance of my little pet of long years ago are two cards upon which are pasted scraps of yarn from which the stockings were knit.[15]

It is certain that Mary Sawyer Tyler visited the "Aunt Tabitha Spinning Bee" in Old South Church on February 13, 1878, and sold some of her fleece cards there. The *Boston Transcript* said so, the next afternoon. But that was all that was ever proved (by anything except her own recollections) about her touching story. When Ford went looking for Mary's school he was shown a nondescript shed that was part of a garage in Sterling. He bought the lumber, and very soon a trim little red schoolhouse was restored—or reincarnated—on the grounds of the Wayside Inn. In front of this the Fords placed two boulders, with bronze plaques attached. On one was reproduced in facsimile the pages from William H. McGuffey's *Second Eclectic Reader* where millions of nineteenth-century schoolchildren—including Henry Ford—learned about Mary and her lamb. McGuffey was no bibliographer, so he did not mention the name of the woman who wrote and published "Mary's Lamb" in a Boston children's magazine, in 1830, over the initials "S. J. H." But the Fords named her on their other boulder, and gave her the credit they thought she deserved: "Sarah Josepha Hale, whose genius completed the poem in its present form." [16]

The "Mary Lamb School" which Ford erected was not just a monument to faulty research: it was also a working school where smaller children of the Inn's staff, and others from the vicinity, attended regular classes. Ford also opened a larger school, for boys only, where orphans and other wards of the Commonwealth received a vocational education at Ford's expense. A gristmill, a sawmill, and a blacksmith-horseshoeing shop demonstrated old American skills and plied them in a productive manner. (The gristmill today is still turning out flour for Pepperidge Farm bread.) There was also a large modern dairy and a canning kitchen with a capacity of 10,000 jars of fruit and jelly a year.[17]

[15] Ford Archives, Acc. 111 (Wayside Inn Papers); "The True Story of Mary's Little Lamb," *Dearborn Independent*, March 19 and 26, 1927. These articles, probably written by W. J. Cameron, were revised and printed in a forty-page book, *The Story of Mary and Her Little Lamb as told by Mary and her Neighbors and Friends. To which is added a critical analysis of the poem.* Published by Mr. and Mrs. Henry Ford (Dearborn, 1928). Ruth E. Finley, *The Lady of Godey's: Sarah Josepha Hale* (Philadelphia and London, 1931), pp. 279–305, provides a devastating critique of the Tyler-Ford-Cameron claims.

[16] *Story of Mary and Her Little Lamb*, pp. 2–3; "Wayside Inn History," p. 64.

[17] Ford Archives, Acc. 1, Box 87, has voluminous reports and diaries kept by the students, which were forwarded to Ford in Dearborn. See also "Wayside Inn History," pp. 64–65; Linton Wells, "A Tale of the Wayside Inn," typescript, Acc. 1, Box 84; Nevins and Hill, *Ford*, pp. 498–99.

Meanwhile the real work of the Inn—entertaining, edifying, and indoctrinating the public—went on with complete success. The firelight gleamed red in Longfellow's parlor, Daniel Webster's desk stood in one corner, and the old "Governor Eustis" coach in which Webster and Lafayette rode off to dedicate Bunker Hill Monument creaked around the grounds from time to time. The ballroom was open for old-fashioned quadrilles, in which the Fords took an agile part. When the former Allegra Longfellow (by then Mrs. Thorpe) complained that the dance floor was not "springy," as she remembered, Ford installed metal springs beneath the boards, "to get back the old elasticity." [18]

The barroom was especially inviting, with its rows of mugs and tankards and flip glasses. But strong drinks were not served during Ford's regime, which lasted through 1945, long after Prohibition expired. Students of early New England customs might cavil at this, and I am sure they did, but they had to be satisfied with a look at President Coolidge's signature, on the bottom of an empty sap bucket from the Coolidge farm in Vermont. Ford, moreover, had poetic precedent for his rumless tavern. It was Longfellow himself who assembled the landlord and six guests—a student, a Spanish Jew, a Sicilian, a Norwegian musician, a theologian, and Harvard poet—and kept them up most of the night in the parlor, reciting the ride of Paul Revere, playing the violin, telling tales and tending the fire—and never gave them a drop to drink! [19]

The absence of alcohol helped make the Inn a favorite stopping place for clergymen and their families. Another attraction was Ford's policy of picking up the tab himself for all charges to men of the cloth. In a typical month he paid, by his personal check, the bills of forty-eight ordained guests, including a Methodist Bishop from New York, and a luncheon party of fifteen priests from Lowell. The total was only $143.05, and I note the liquorless lunches cost as little as 75 cents. Ford, as landlord, paid similar bills twelve times each year during twenty-three years. [20]

These amounts were trivial when compared to his total outlay. For the Inn itself, and ninety acres of land, he paid $65,000 to begin with. The other properties, remodeling and furnishing, road changing, school moving, and so forth, ran up his capital expenditures to the much grander sum of $1,616,956.11. In addition he incurred operating losses in amounts ranging from $40,000 to $180,000 a year, and totaling $2,848,187.27. So in all the Inn cost Ford around $4,500,000.

Ford begrudged not a cent of it; he was continuously delighted with what he made of the Inn. And so were most of his guests. The best proof

[18] "Wayside Inn History," pp. 60–61; "Henry Ford: Why I Bought the Wayside Inn," pp. 42–45.

[19] Henry Wadsworth Longfellow, *Tales of a Wayside Inn* (Boston, 1863).

[20] "Re Wayside Inn," which also lists room and meal charges for clergymen in November, 1945.

of this came in 1955—eight years after Ford died—when fire destroyed the original Inn, and almost everything he had put into it. That same afternoon the *Christian Science Monitor*, in its news report of the fire, virtually decreed that the Inn must rise from its ashes.

"The question immediately arises," said the *Monitor*, "whether the Inn will be rebuilt. The property is owned by the Ford Foundation, which has *as yet*[*] issued no statement of its intentions. Certainly the thousands who have enjoyed the warm hospitality of this historic site will cherish the hope that restoration, perhaps along the lines of Colonial Williamsburg, can be undertaken." [21]

The *Monitor's* information was not correct; the Inn was never owned by the Ford Foundation. In 1944 it was transferred by Ford to a Massachusetts charitable corporation, named "The Wayside Inn." [22] And it was not tactful to point to Colonial Williamsburg, a late starter in Ford's estimation. But the *Monitor's* wishes were authentically Boston's, and were soon reinforced by the Massachusetts General Court, which passed an encouraging resolution, and by a coin-collecting campaign among schoolchildren that extended to Hawaii and Chile. The Ford Foundation responded nobly, I think; within two months it set aside $500,000 to replace the Inn.[23] Later it gave more money to buy more antique furniture. The Inn since 1960 has been administered by Boston trustees; it now earns enough to pay its expenses. It offers the public historical atmosphere, conventional meals at sensible prices, and a choice of exotic colonial drinks, including stonewall cocktails, meetinghouse punch, and a mixture called "coow woow." [24]

Ford's matured concept of history as the appreciation and study of "the general resourcefulness of our people" [25] lives on in the vast collections and the more than 100 buildings of the Henry Ford Museum-Greenfield Village-Edison Institute complex at Dearborn. This has become by far the most popular historical preserve in the United States (under nongovernmental operation). Its entertainment features are conspicuous, but its basic purpose is mass education. The Museum exhibits classified arts, tools, machines, and products; the Village arranges them in old houses and workshops (including fifty-one "transplanted originals") in ways they

---

[*]Italics supplied. The embers still glowed when this was written. [R. B.]

[21] *Christian Science Monitor*, December 22, 1955; *The New York Times*, December 23, 1955.

[22] Henry S. Streeter, secretary of the corporation, to the present writer, November 3, 1965.

[23] *Journal of American Insurance* (September 1961); *The New York Times*, February 19, 1956. The Inn was reopened in June, 1958.

[24] Menu and drink card of "Longfellow's Wayside Inn," 1965.

[25] Henry Ford, "The Idea Behind Greenfield," as told to Arthur Van Vlissingen, Jr., *American Legion Monthly*, October, 1932, p. 50.

were once used and lived with; the Institute is strictly a school.[26] The research facilities of these institutions were augmented in 1965 by the 14 million letters, documents, photographs, and other items in the personal and office archives of Henry Ford, certain members of his family, many of his associates and competitors, and of the Ford Motor Company down to recent years. Outside all this is Ford's wealth itself, embodied in the Ford Foundation, which supplied the funds to continue editing the Adams Papers owned by this Society, and also those of Jefferson, Hamilton, Franklin, and Madison.[27]

It is all a remarkable legacy from the man who said—excuse me, who did not say—"History is bunk." [28]

[26] "Comparative Museum Attendance, December, 1964," issued monthly by Old Sturbridge Village; *Antiques at the Ford Museum*, by the editors of Antiques Magazine (New York, 1958); "The Past is Present at Greenfield Village," *National Geographic*, July, 1958, pp. 96–127.

[27] "Appraisal of the Ford Motor Company Archives, Dearborn, Michigan" (Pittsburgh: Industrial Appraisal Company, 1964), p. ii, *et passim; The New York Times*, October 21, 1964.

[28] Ford's exact words, "History is more or less bunk," are correctly stated in two collections of quotations I have consulted: *The Great Quotations*, comp. George Seldes (New York, 1960) and Henry F. Woods, *American Sayings* (New York, 1945). In *A New Dictionary of Quotations on Historical Principles* (New York, 1942), H. L. Mencken gives the familiar folklore version but offers a sceptical discussion. Four other works are incorrect and give no discussion: *The Oxford Dictionary of Quotations*, 2nd ed. (London, 1955); John Bartlett, *Familiar Quotations*, 11th ed. (Boston, 1939); Burton Stevenson, *The Home Book of Quotations*, 9th ed. (New York, 1958); and Herbert V. Prochnow and Herbert V. Prochnow, Jr., *A Dictionary of Wit, Wisdom & Satire* (New York, 1962).

19

John B. Rae: "Ford Still Defies Interpretation"[1]

For all the millions of words that have been written about Henry Ford and the Model T, much of the story of the innovation of full-fledged mass production by the Ford Motor Company remains fragmentary. Ford himself still defies interpretation: mechanical genius (probably) but woefully ignorant in most other matters; visionary, sometimes shrewdly so and sometimes incredibly naive; and completely imbued with the attitudes and prejudices of nineteenth-century rural America. It is impossible to say when he first had the idea of a "car for the great multitude," or more specifically, as he sometimes said, a car to help the farmer. His own reminiscences have to be disregarded. Except where machinery was concerned, Henry Ford's thought processes were seldom logical, and he had the human propensity for remembering things the way he wanted them to be.

The first models offered by the Ford Motor Company after its establishment in 1903 were definitely not aimed at the low-priced market. They were competitive in the medium-price range ($1,000–$1,500) with cars like Buick and Maxwell-Briscoe. At the same time Ford's quarrel with Malcomson, insofar as it involved a policy issue and not simply Henry Ford's distaste for any rival in the control of his company, appears to have stemmed from Ford's desire to experiment with a low-priced car. It is clear that Ford had definitely set his sights on the mass market and knew what must be done to reach it. In 1903 he told one of his partners, John W. Anderson, "The way to make automobiles is to make one automobile like another automobile, to make them all alike, to make them come from the factory just alike—just like one pin is like another pin when it comes from a pin factory."

Henry Ford succeeded where others failed, principally because, instead of starting out to produce a car as cheaply as possible, he concentrated first on designing a car that would be suitable for the mass market and

[1] From John B. Rae, *The American Automobile* (Chicago: University of Chicago Press, 1965), pp. 58–60, 62–63, 77–79, 164. Copyright © 1965 by the University of Chicago. Reprinted by permission of the University of Chicago Press.

then turned his attention to the problem of cutting manufacturing costs. There is nothing to suggest that he himself was consciously aware of the significance of this two-step progression; if he grasped it he did so intuitively. Low price was only one of the characteristics required in an automobile intended for use by the general public. It also had to be durable, easy to operate so that it could be driven by any ordinary individual, economical to maintain, and simple to repair—preferably simple enough for the owner to do most of the maintenance and repairs himself. After some experimentation these qualities were achieved in 1907 with the Model T—the "flivver," or "Tin Lizzie,"—the most famous motor vehicle ever built. First offered to the public in 1908, it had a rugged body, mounted high to enable it to negotiate country roads. Its twenty-horsepower four-cylinder engine was a marvel of mechanical simplicity, as was its planetary transmission, which had two speeds forward and one in reverse and required only the pressing or releasing of foot-pedals to operate. Some of the strength in its construction was achieved by using alloy steels, an innovation in American practice although European automobile builders had been using them for some time. Ford, in fact, was responsible for introducing the manufacture of vanadium steel to the United States, since the market for it had previously been so small that American steel firms did not consider it worth producing.

The basic concept of the "car for the great multitude" and the qualities it ought to have was definitely Henry Ford's. In the design of the car itself he contributed a good deal but has to share credit with others, conspicuously C. H. (for Childe Harold) Wills (1878–1940), who was the proponent of alloy steels, and Joseph Galamb, who worked out many of the mechanical features of the Model T. Only Ford himself, however, could have taken the next step along the way; namely, the decision in 1909 that the Ford Motor Company should give up all its other models and concentrate exclusively on the production of the Model T. The achievement of full-scale mass production was enough in itself to give Henry Ford his place in history. His assembly-line technique was crude by present-day standards, but to an astonished world it was a miracle of production to have Model T Fords, all identical in engine and chassis, pour off the assembly line at the rate of one every three minutes. By 1920 every other motor vehicle in the world was a Model T Ford, and the Ford Motor Company simply had no competition in its price class.

But that was not all. Simultaneously with the appearance of the complete assembly line came the announcement of a basic wage rate at the Ford Motor Company of five dollars a day, approximately twice the going rate in Detroit at the time. This announcement likewise drew world-wide attention to Ford, besides giving consternation to a good many business leaders. Job seekers converged on Detroit by the thousand; in fact, shortly after the new policy was put in effect, fire hoses had to be used to disperse the mob of applicants around the Highland Park plant. There was some fine print in the contract. Ford employees had to work for six months to become eligible for the five-dollar rate and even after that had to be "worthy" of it.

The precise origin of the five-dollar day is as much a mystery as that of the moving assembly line. Part of the motive behind it was a desire to reduce the high turnover in the company's labor force, and for this purpose James S. Couzens was interested in raising wages. Again, however, the final decision had to be made by Henry Ford. The five-dollar figure— simple and dramatic—came from the flair for publicity that he possessed to an unusual degree. Beyond this, and more important as a contributing factor, was Ford's own philosophy of business. He believed that the gains made by improving techniques of production should be passed on to society as a whole in three ways: to stockholders in the conventional form of dividends, to consumers in the form of lower prices, and to labor in the form of higher wages.

In Ford's mind this was undoubtedly an intuitive concept rather than a logical body of thought—the rationalizing was done for him later by others—but it was still as revolutionary in its implications for the economic structure of capitalism as the assembly line was for its technological development. He was the first man not only to preach but to practice the doctrine that the buying public had a legitimate interest in the operations of a big business organization, and he grasped a vital aspect of the relationship of mass consumption to mass production; namely, that labor is something more than a commodity to be procured at the lowest possible cost. The worker is also a consumer. For this reason a distinguished French observer of American society, R. L. Bruckberger, insists in *The Image of America* that for the twentieth century Ford's revolution is far more important than Lenin's.

*   *   *

This period [the early 1920's], indeed, was the high noon of Henry Ford's career. His feat in revolutionizing motor vehicle production was still reasonably fresh, and there was so far no near rival. To the great bulk of the American people (and many others) he was the mechanical wizard with the Midas touch, the Horatio Alger hero who had climbed from farm boy to billionaire by his own unaided genius. He became a sort of Paul Bunyan figure, for whom no task was too great. The most vivid illustration of the Ford legend appears in a Pullman smoking room conversation during the early twenties, overheard and reported by Frederic L. Smith, former president of the Olds Motor Works, in *Motoring Down a Quarter of a Century* (Detroit, 1928):

"Who invented the automobile anyway?"

"Henry Ford. Started as a racer by beating Barney Oldfield on the ice at Detroit. Right after that he built a plant to turn out the same kind of car in fifty thousand lots."

"Doesn't he own the Lincoln now?"

"Yeah, owns the Lincoln and the Packard, Cadillac, Buick—all the big ones and a lot of the little ones besides."

"Is it true about his taking over the Detroit City Hospital?"

"I'll say it's true. Bought it and runs it for his employees. Charges everybody a fixed rate for every job and makes it pay."

Among the inaccuracies, the reference to the hospital does less than justice to the Henry Ford Hospital in Dearborn.

It is now a forgotten item of American history that Henry Ford was a Democratic candidate for the office of United States Senator from Michigan in 1918 and lost by a narrow margin to Truman S. Newberry, who was subsequently deprived of his seat because of election frauds. Had Ford won, the Senate in 1919 would have been divided equally between Democrats and Republicans, 48-48, so that with the tie-breaking vote of Vice President Marshall the Democrats would have controlled the chamber. In this situation the chairman of the Committee on Foreign Relations during the debate on the Versailles Treaty and the League of Nations would have been a Democrat and not Henry Cabot Lodge the elder. In this respect it was a significant election; what Henry Ford would have been like as a senator otherwise has to be left to speculation. As a popular idol he was inevitably mentioned as a presidential prospect, and in the early 1920's an organized movement came into existence to give him the Republican nomination in 1924. This however was stopped, after some hesitation, by Ford himself.

For Henry Ford, and still more for his family and friends, the attraction of public life was markedly lessened by his experience when he sued the *Chicago Tribune* for libel for calling him "an ignorant idealist" and "an anarchistic enemy of the nation." The objectionable editorial appeared in 1916, when the *Tribune* and Ford were in sharp difference over the desirability of military preparedness, but the case did not come to trial until 1919. Henry Ford was put on the witness stand for a pitiless exposure of his ignorance of nonautomotive subjects. He did not, however, actually say "History is bunk." What he did say was that when he was in school he thought that history was bunk, which is quite a different thing and in fact a fairly common educational experience. Yet, however unpleasant this incident might have been, it did not diminish the glamour of the Ford name in the least. If anything, the effect was just the opposite. The intelligentsia might sneer, but they made their usual blunder of believing that what they thought was public opinion. The average American knew

just as little history as Henry Ford and had much the same opinion of it.
Ford's deficiencies made him more than ever a figure with whom the
common man could feel an affinity: clearly a titan, but equally clearly
molded from common clay. Aldous Huxley meant it as satire, but he was
hitting very close to the mark when he made Ford the deity of *Brave New
World*.

*   *   *

It took time and effort to wear down old Henry's reluctance to surrender
his control, but it was finally achieved, and on September 21, 1945, Henry
Ford II was elected president of the Ford Motor Company, with a free
hand to manage it as he chose. Harry Bennett received his walking papers
the same day, although he was given a month to wind up his affairs, which
was a greater courtesy than he had extended to the innumerable victims
of the Bennett ascendancy. The founder of the company went into complete retirement for the two years more that he had to live, a senile invalid
with his great days far behind him.

It was a tragic end to a phenomenal career. For good or ill, Henry Ford
was the image of America to millions of people throughout the world, and
on balance it was a favorable image. He was not just the poor boy who
became enormously rich; he was the prophet who struck the rock of mass
production and brought from it a stream of plenty for rich and poor alike,
who made luxuries like motorcars accessible to the common man, and who
saw the secret of prosperity in wages high enough to leave the wage-earner
with disposable income. If he was a despot, in his early days he was a
benevolent one and for his great achievements he could be forgiven some
foibles and eccentricities. Had he been willing to turn over real authority
to Edsel and retire along with the Model T, his reputation would be
unassailable. Instead he stayed on, dominated by the prejudices of his
rural boyhood and unable to adapt to a fast-changing industrial society
which he had done as much as anyone to create; unwilling to let anyone
else run his company and progressively less able to do it himself. It is not
really surprising that the news of his death startled a good many people
because they were under the impression that it had occurred some time
before.

Bibliographical Note

The considerable volume of publication attributed to Henry Ford is, as was stated in the text, of uncertain value. The actual writing was done by others, and Ford's testimony in both the Dodge and *Chicago Tribune* cases makes it evident that he seldom read what appeared in print under his name. He had three books published in collaboration with Samuel Crowther: *My Life and Work* (Garden City, New York, 1922), *Today and Tomorrow* (Garden City, 1926), and *Moving Forward* (Garden City, 1931). These can be accepted as reasonably faithful expressions of Henry Ford's ideas, along with the interviews with F. L. Faurote, *My Philosophy of Industry* (New York, 1929). Ford also had his own page in the *Dearborn Independent*, and some of these articles are collected in *Ford Ideas* (Dearborn, Michigan, 1926). They were actually written by William J. Cameron, but it can be taken for granted that Cameron adhered closely to his employer's views.

Biographies are innumerable. Of those written during Ford's lifetime, it is noticeable that the adulatory ones were written before the coming of the Depression. These include A. L. Benson, *The New Henry Ford* (New York, 1923); Sarah Bushnell, *The Truth about Henry Ford* (Chicago, 1922); J. de Roulhac Hamilton, *Henry Ford* (New York, 1927), by a well-known historical scholar; and Charles Merz, *And Then Came Ford* (Garden City, New York, 1929). In the 1930's the field was held by Ford's critics, typified by J. N. Leonard, *The Tragedy of Henry Ford* (New York, 1932), and Upton Sinclair's novel *The Flivver King* (Detroit, 1937). Gamaliel Bradford, *The Quick and the Dead* (Boston, 1931), a collection of essays by an eminent literary critic, has a reasonably balanced appraisal of Ford.

Subsequent biographical work is dominated by the three-volume study by Allan Nevins and F. E. Hill: *Ford: The Times, the Man, the Company* (New York, 1954); *Ford: Expansion and Challenge 1915-1932* (New York, 1957); and *Ford: Decline and Rebirth 1933-1962* (New York, 1963). Roger Burlingame, *Henry Ford. A Great Life in Brief* (New York, 1955), and Keith Sward, *The Legend of Henry Ford* (New York, 1948), both cited in the text, are excellent single-volume studies. There is also Garet Garrett, *The Wild Wheel* (New York, 1952), by a journalist who had a long association with Ford. Harry Bennett, *We Never Called Him Henry* (New York, 1951) is not especially valuable, but Charles E. Sorensen, *My Forty Years with Ford* (New York, 1956) is illuminating on several important aspects of Ford history. William Greenleaf, *Monopoly on Wheels* (Detroit, 1961), is the authority on Ford and the Selden patent, and the international expansion of the Ford business is recounted in detail in Myra Wilkins and F. E. Hill, *American Business Abroad: Ford on Six Continents* (Detroit, 1964).

There are useful insights on Ford in works dealing with his associates and competitors. Especially recommended are Norman Beasley, *Knudsen. A Biography* (New York, 1947); Walter P. Chrysler, in collaboration with Boyden Sparks, *Life of an American Workman* (New York, 1937); Mrs. Wilfred G. Leland, with M. D. Millbrook, *Master of Precision. Henry M. Leland* (Detroit, 1966); Alfred Lief, *The Firestone Story* (New York, 1951)—Harvey Firestone was a close friend of Henry Ford; A. P. Sloan, Jr., *My Years with General Motors* (New York, 1964); and F. L. Smith, *Motoring Down a Quarter of a Century* (Detroit, 1928). Other personal reminiscences of Henry Ford appear in E. W. Lewis, *Motor Memories* (Detroit, 1947), and C. G. Sinsabaugh, *Who, Me? Forty Years of Automobile History* (Detroit, 1940).

An accurate perspective on Henry Ford requires an understanding of the history of the American automobile industry as a whole. For this the following can be recommended: R. E. Anderson, *The Story of the American Automobile* (Washington, D. C., 1950); R. M. Cleveland and S. T. Williamson, *The Road Is Yours* (New York, 1951); D. L. Cohn, *Combustion on Wheels* (Boston, 1944); Merrill Denison, *The Power to Go* (Garden City, New York, 1956); R. C. Epstein, *The Automobile Industry* (Chicago, 1928); C. B. Glasscock, *The Gasoline Age* (Indianapolis, 1937); E. D. Kennedy, *The Automobile Industry* (New York, 1941); T. F. MacManus and Norman Beasley, *Men, Money, and Motors* (New York, 1929); J. B. Rae, *American Automobile Manufacturers: The First Forty Years* (Philadelphia, 1959) and *The American Automobile* (Chicago, 1965); and L. H. Seltzer, *Financial History of the American Automobile Industry* (Boston, 1928).

Three studies of special fields deserve attention: business organization in A. D. Chandler, *Ford, General Motors, and the Automobile Industry* (New York, 1964); labor relations in Sidney Fine, *The Automobile under the Blue Eagle* (Ann Arbor, Michigan, 1963); and dealer relationships in Stewart Macaulay, *Law and the Balance of Power—The Automobile Manufacturers and their Dealers* (New York, 1966).

Index

GREAT LIVES OBSERVED

Gerald Emanuel Stearn, *General Editor*

Other volumes in the series:

Churchill, edited by Martin Gilbert

Cromwell, edited by Maurice Ashley

Frederick Douglass, edited by Benjamin Quarles

Garibaldi, edited by Denis Mack Smith

William Lloyd Garrison, edited by George M. Fredrickson

Hitler, edited by George H. Stein

Jesus, edited by Hugh Anderson

La Follette, edited by Robert S. Maxwell

Lloyd George, edited by Martin Gilbert

Mao, edited by Jerome Ch'en

Robespierre, edited by George Rude

Franklin Delano Roosevelt, edited by Gerald D. Nash

Stalin, edited by T. H. Rigby

Booker T. Washington, edited by Emma Lou Thornbrough